# C O N T E

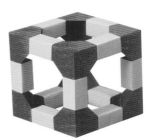

All model titles are also given in Japanese for the reader's reference.

# Folding Symbols

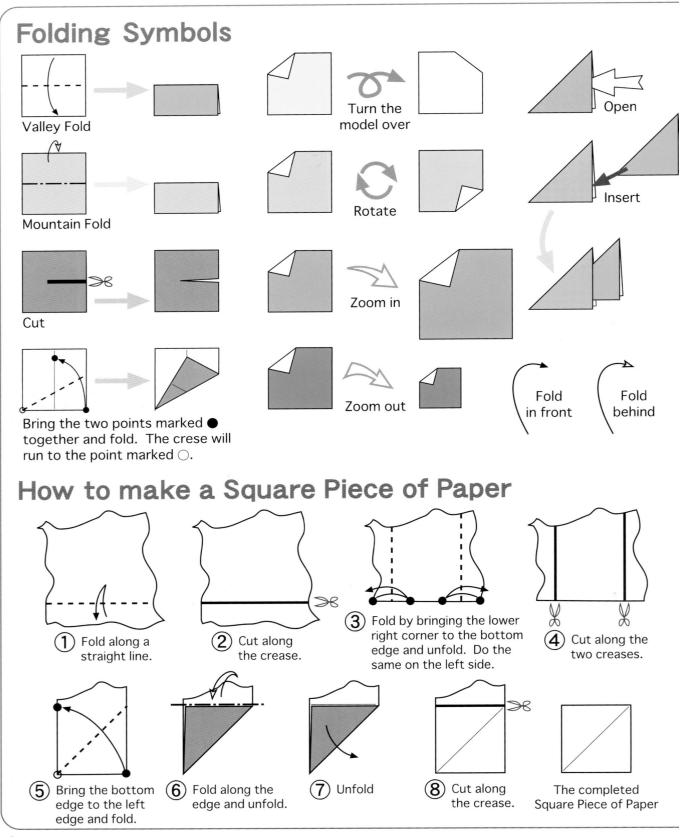

Valley Fold

Mountain Fold

Cut

Bring the two points marked ● together and fold. The crese will run to the point marked ○.

Turn the model over

Rotate

Zoom in

Zoom out

Open

Insert

Fold in front

Fold behind

# How to make a Square Piece of Paper

① Fold along a straight line.

② Cut along the crease.

③ Fold by bringing the lower right corner to the bottom edge and unfold. Do the same on the left side.

④ Cut along the two creases.

⑤ Bring the bottom edge to the left edge and fold.

⑥ Fold along the edge and unfold.

⑦ Unfold

⑧ Cut along the crease.

The completed Square Piece of Paper

# A Note about Folding and Assembly

- For easy folding, always fold on a flat, firm surface.

- If you cannot understand a diagram, try to look ahead to the next diagram to see what the result is supposed to look like.

- When you fold a piece of paper, you should line up corners, edges and creases very carefully. Neatness is important!

- When you make a crease, always turn the model so you are folding the corner or flap away from you, as in the example to the right. This way you can see the crease while you're folding it.

- Once you've folded a model from one type or color of paper, try folding it again with something different!

- Example: How to fold into a triangle.

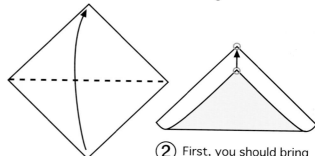

① This diagram means fold the paper in half.

② First, you should bring the bottom corner up to the top corner and line them up exactly.

③ Second, you hold the part marked ★ with one hand. Then you squash the bottom edge with the other hand from the center to the right corner.

④ Do the same on the left side, switching hands.

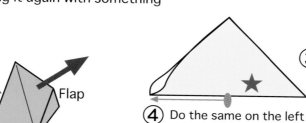

Pocket

Flap

- Example: A module

Flap

Pocket

- You will make some geometrical models by putting many modules together. Usually a module has both flaps and pockets. To join, you tuck a flap of a module into a pocket of another module.

- When you assemble modules into a model, you should tuck the flaps into the pockets one by one.

- If you want to strengthen a model, you can put glue on the face of a flap and then insert it into its pocket.

- Tucking the last flap into the last pocket is the most difficult step in the assembly of a model. You should open the model up a little and insert the flap carefully.

- For easy assembly of models with many pieces, start by using 3"~ 5" pieces of square paper. After you have gained some experience, you can try them with different-sized paper.

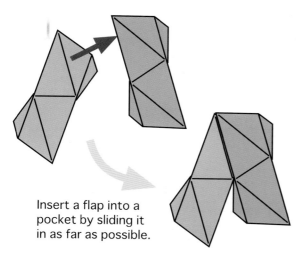

Insert a flap into a pocket by sliding it in as far as possible.

# TILES

## SQUARE TILE 1
●Diagram: Page 92

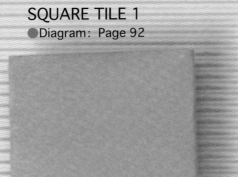

## RIGHT TRIANGULAR TILE
●Diagram: Page 93

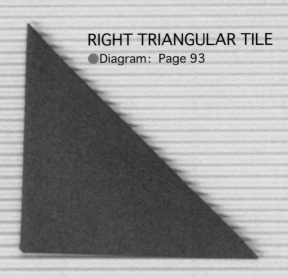

## ISOSCELES TRIANGULAR TILE
●Diagram: Page 93

## RECTANGULAR TILE 1
●Diagram: Page 92

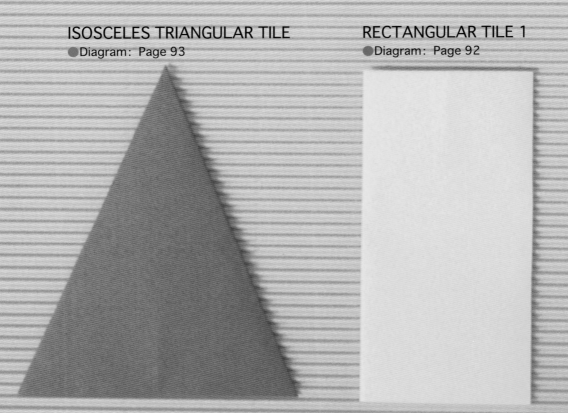

Front

## EQUILATERAL
## TRIANGULAR TILE
●Diagram: Page 96

## SQUARE TILE 2
●Diagram: Page 94

## REGULAR
## PENTAGONAL TILE
●Diagram: Page 98

## REGULAR
## HEXAGONAL TILE
●Diagram: Page 97

## RHOMBIC TILE
●Diagram: Page 96

## RECTANGULAR TILE 2
●Diagram: Page 94

## REGULAR
## OCTAGONAL TILE
●Diagram: Page 95

Back

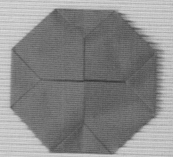

# BRICKS
Diagram: Page 10

# BRICK れんが レンガ
## RE - N - GA

Start with a square piece of paper.

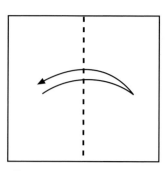

① Fold in half and unfold.

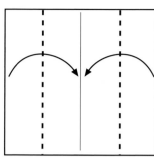

② Bring the right edge to the center line and fold. Do the same on the left side.

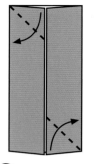

③ Fold only the upper layer.

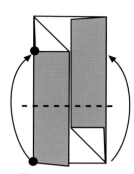

④ Bring the two points marked ● together and fold.

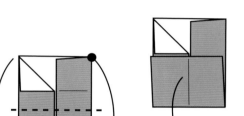

⑤ Fold along the edge and unfold.

⑥ Unfold.

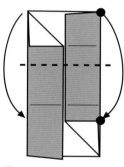

⑦ Bring the two points marked ● together and fold.

⑧ Fold along the edge and unfold.

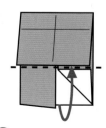

⑨ Tuck the flap into the pocket.

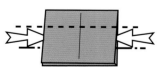

⑩ Open to form a brick. Use existing creases.

The completed
BRICK

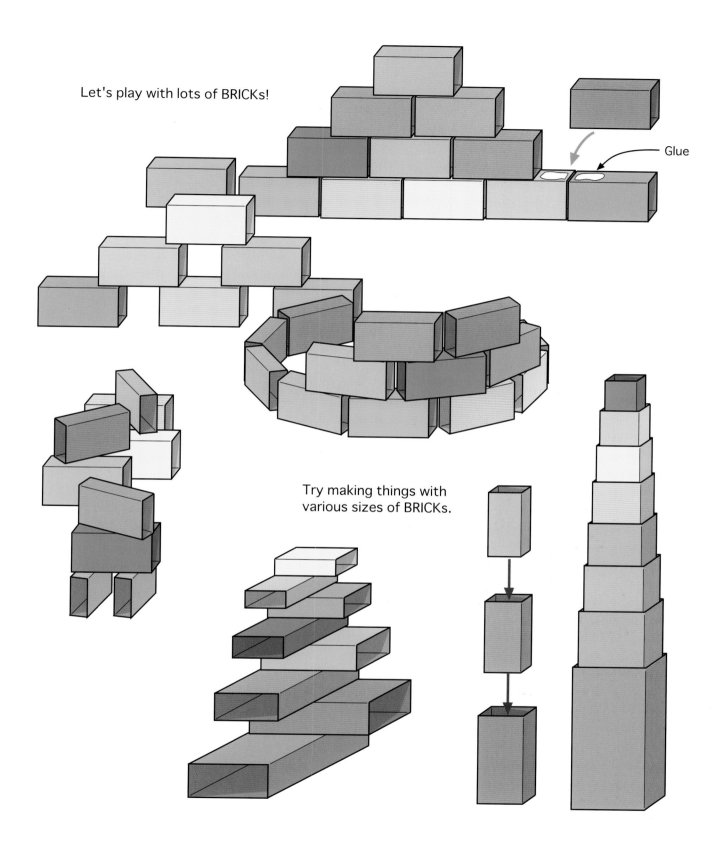

Let's play with lots of BRICKs!

Glue

Try making things with
various sizes of BRICKs.

# RIGHT CORNERS

### RIGHT CORNER 1
● Diagram: Page 13

### RIGHT CORNER 3
● Diagram: Page 14

### RIGHT CORNER 2
● Diagram: Page 14

## Arrangements of Right Corners

# RIGHT CORNER 1

ちょっかくこ ー な ー いち
## 直角コーナー 1
*CHOK-KAKU KO - O - NA - A  ICHI*

Start with a square piece of paper.

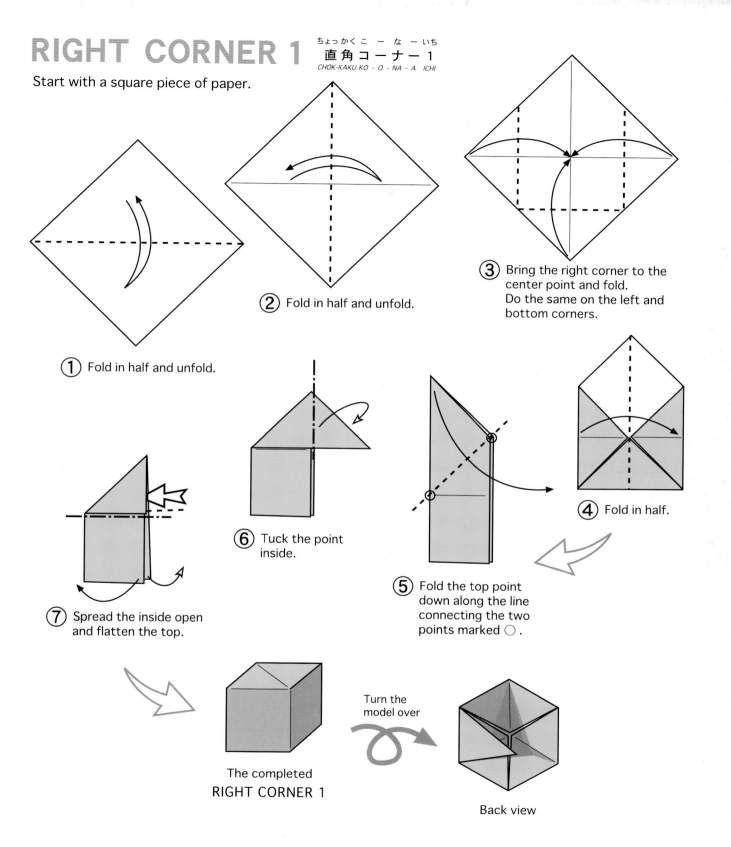

① Fold in half and unfold.

② Fold in half and unfold.

③ Bring the right corner to the center point and fold. Do the same on the left and bottom corners.

④ Fold in half.

⑤ Fold the top point down along the line connecting the two points marked ○ .

⑥ Tuck the point inside.

⑦ Spread the inside open and flatten the top.

The completed
RIGHT CORNER 1

Turn the model over

Back view

# RIGHT CORNER 2 直角コーナー2

ちょっかくこ ー なー に
*CHOK-KAKU KO - O - NA - A NI*

Start with a square piece of paper.

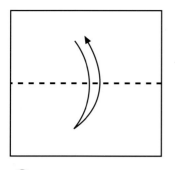

① Fold in half and unfold.

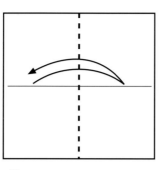

② Fold in half and unfold.

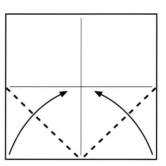

③ Bring the lower right corner to the center point and fold. Do the same on the left side.

④ Fold by bringing each corner to the center point and unfold.

# RIGHT CORNER 3 直角コーナー3

ちょっかくこ ー な ー さん
*CHOK-KAKU KO - O - NA - A SAN*

Start with a square piece of paper.

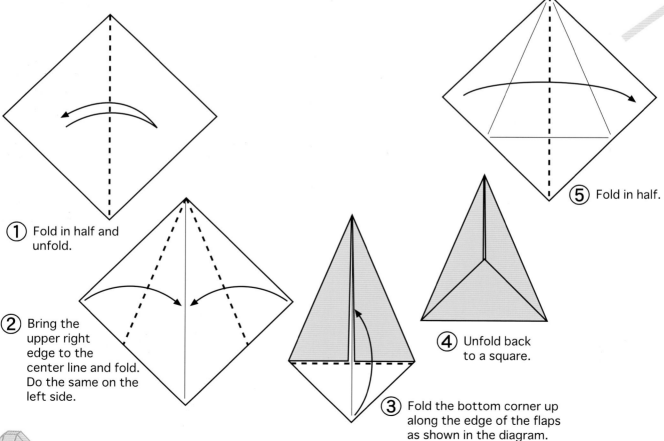

① Fold in half and unfold.

② Bring the upper right edge to the center line and fold. Do the same on the left side.

③ Fold the bottom corner up along the edge of the flaps as shown in the diagram.

④ Unfold back to a square.

⑤ Fold in half.

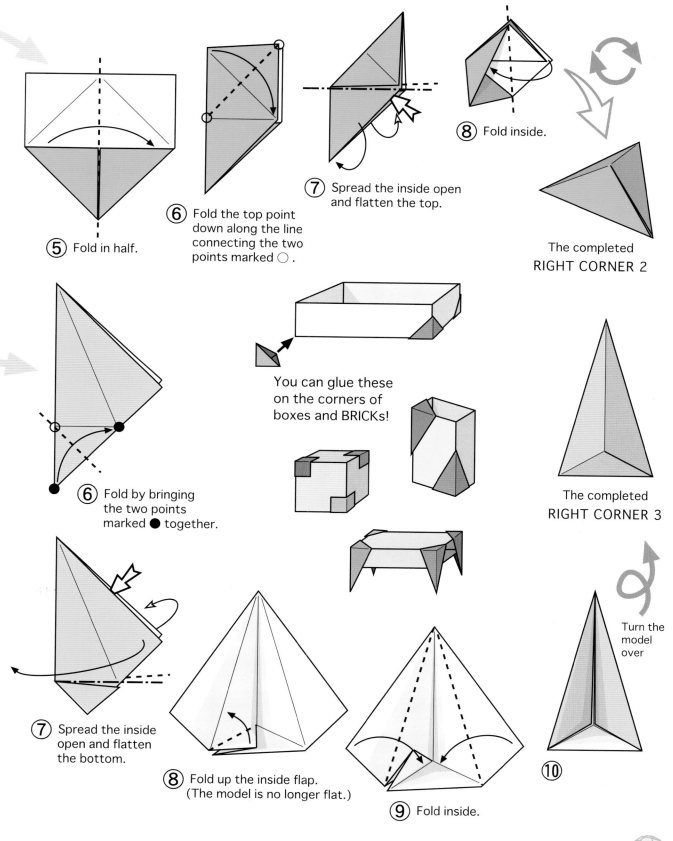

⑤ Fold in half.

⑥ Fold the top point down along the line connecting the two points marked ○ .

⑦ Spread the inside open and flatten the top.

⑧ Fold inside.

The completed
RIGHT CORNER 2

⑥ Fold by bringing the two points marked ● together.

You can glue these on the corners of boxes and BRICKs!

The completed
RIGHT CORNER 3

⑦ Spread the inside open and flatten the bottom.

⑧ Fold up the inside flap. (The model is no longer flat.)

⑨ Fold inside.

⑩

Turn the model over

# PRISM 角柱
かく ちゅう
*KAKU-CHUU*

- A prism is a polyhedron whose top and bottom faces are parallel and identical. The other sides are quadrilaterals.

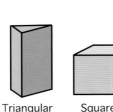  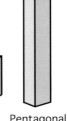   

Triangular Prism　Square Prism　Pentagonal Prism　Hexagonal Prism　Prism　Prism

# ANTIPRISM 反角柱
はん かく ちゅう
*HAN-KAKU-CHUU*

- An antiprism is a polyhedron whose top and bottom faces are parallel and identical. The other sides are triangles.

Triangular Antiprism　Square Antiprism　Pentagonal Antiprism　Hexagonal Antiprism　Antiprism　Antiprism

# PYRAMID 角錐
かく すい
*KAKU - SUI*

- A pyramid is a polyhedron with a polygonal bottom face. The other faces are triangles which meet at a point at the top.

  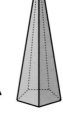   

Triangular Pyramid　Square Pyramid　Pentagonal Pyramid　Hexagonal Pyramid　Pyramid　Pyramid

# DIPYRAMID 両角錐
りょう かく すい
*RYOU-KAKU - SUI*

- A dipyramid is made from two pyramids which have been joined at their bases.

Triangular Dipyramid　Square Dipyramid　Pentagonal Dipyramid　Hexagonal Dipyramid　Dipyramid　Dipyramid

# PRISMS

## TRIANGULAR PRISM
●Diagram: Page 17

## SQUARE PRISM
●Diagram: Page 18

## PENTAGONAL PRISM
●Diagram: Page 18

## HEXAGONAL PRISM
●Diagram: Page 18

# TRIANGULAR PRISM　さん かく ちゅう 3 角 柱
*SAN-KAKU-CHUU*

Start with a square piece of paper.

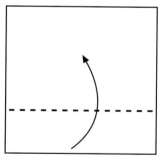

① Fold at about the quarter line.

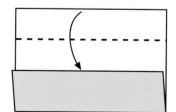

② Bring the top edge down to the other edge of the paper and fold.

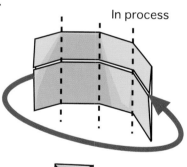

In process

The completed
**TRIANGULAR PRISM**

③ Fold in half and unfold.

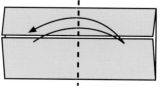

④ Fold along the quarter line and unfold.

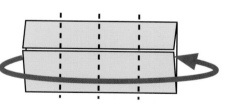

⑥ Tuck one flap inside the other end.

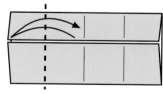

⑤ Fold along the quarter line and unfold.

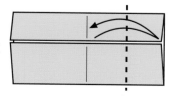

# SQUARE PRISM 4 角柱

しかくちゅう
SHI - KAKU-CHUU

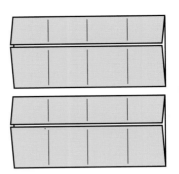

You will need 2 pieces
from step ⑤ on page 17
for each model.

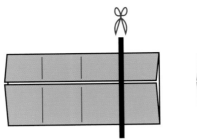 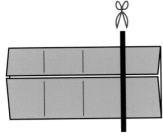

⑦ Cut one flap off each piece.

# PENTAGONAL PRISM 5 角柱

ごかくちゅう
GO - KAKU-CHUU

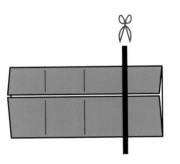
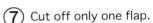

⑦ Cut off only one flap.

# HEXAGONAL PRISM 6 角柱

ろっかくちゅう
ROK-KAKU-CHUU

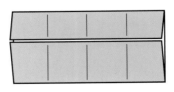 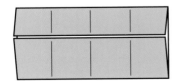

⑦

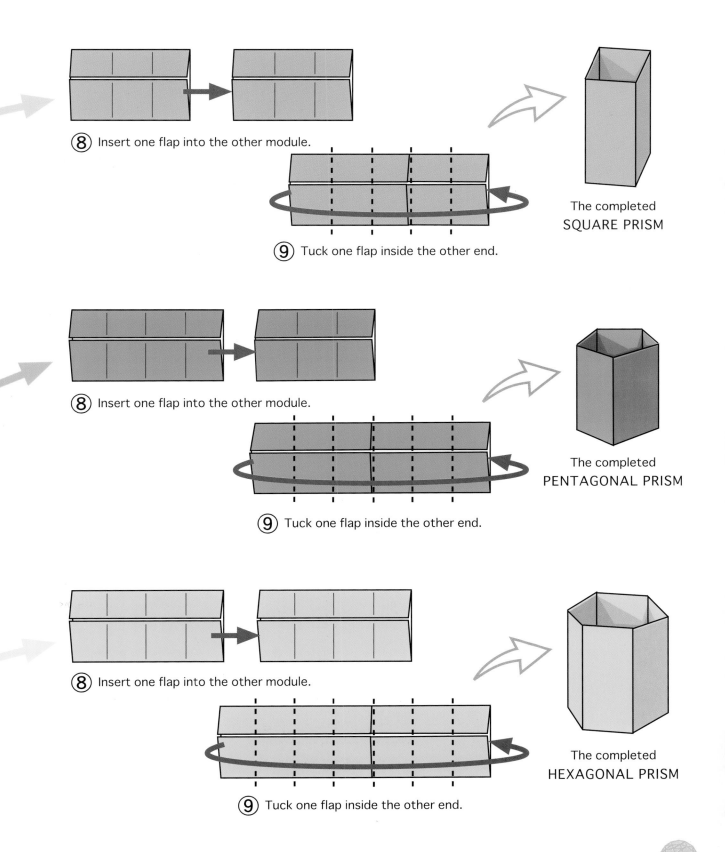

(8) Insert one flap into the other module.

(9) Tuck one flap inside the other end.

The completed
SQUARE PRISM

(8) Insert one flap into the other module.

(9) Tuck one flap inside the other end.

The completed
PENTAGONAL PRISM

(8) Insert one flap into the other module.

(9) Tuck one flap inside the other end.

The completed
HEXAGONAL PRISM

# ANTIPRISMS

**TRIANGULAR
ANTIPRISM**
Diagram: Page 21

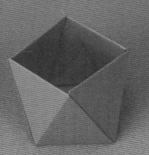

**SQUARE
ANTIPRISM**
Diagram: Page 22

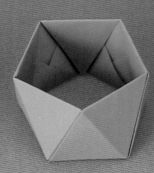

**PENTAGONAL
ANTIPRISM**
Diagram: Page 22

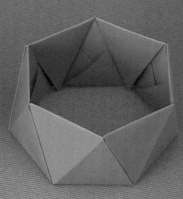

**HEXAGONAL
ANTIPRISM**
Diagram: Page 22

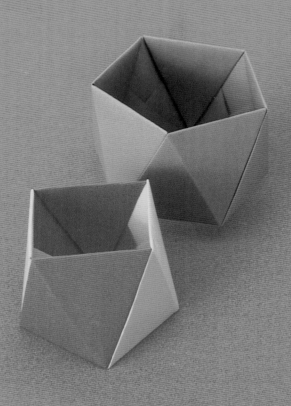

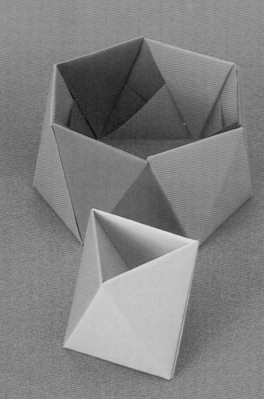

# TRIANGULAR ANTIPRISM

はん さん かく ちゅう
反 3 角 柱
HAN - SAN - KAKU - CHUU

You need 3 square pieces of paper, all the same size.

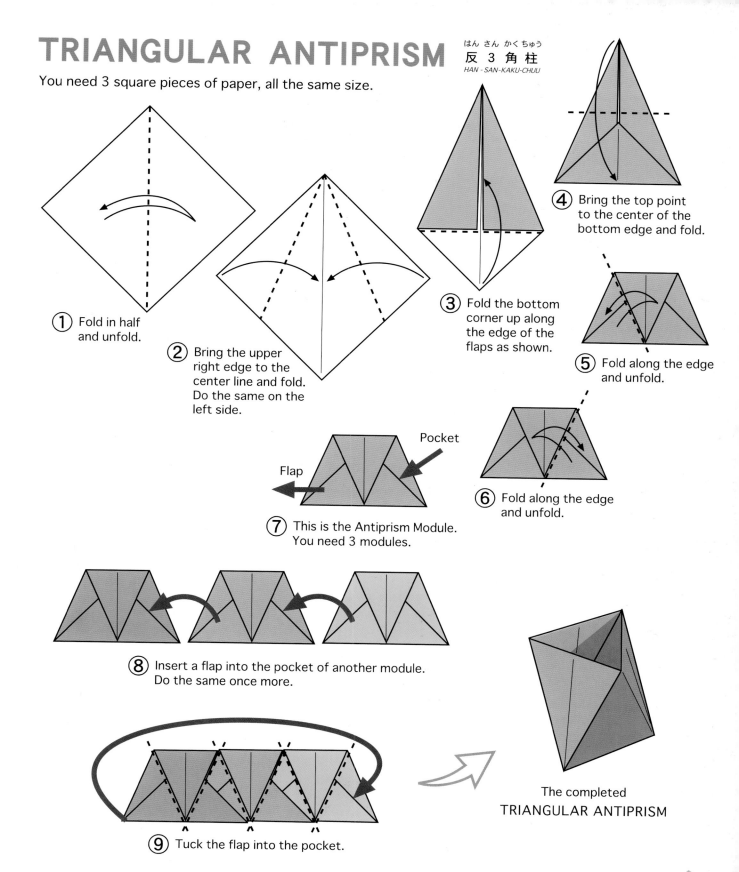

① Fold in half and unfold.

② Bring the upper right edge to the center line and fold. Do the same on the left side.

③ Fold the bottom corner up along the edge of the flaps as shown.

④ Bring the top point to the center of the bottom edge and fold.

⑤ Fold along the edge and unfold.

⑥ Fold along the edge and unfold.

Pocket

Flap

⑦ This is the Antiprism Module. You need 3 modules.

⑧ Insert a flap into the pocket of another module. Do the same once more.

⑨ Tuck the flap into the pocket.

The completed
TRIANGULAR ANTIPRISM

# SQUARE ANTIPRISM

はん し かく ちゅう
反 4 角 柱
*HAN - SHI - KAKU-CHUU*

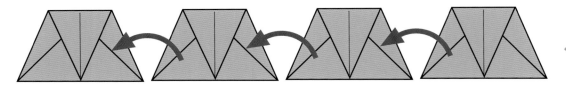

You need 4 Antiprism Modules from page 21.
Insert a flap into the pocket of another module and do
the same two more times. Then tuck the flap into the
pocket at the other end.

The completed
SQUARE
ANTIPRISM

# PENTAGONAL ANTIPRISM

はん ご かく ちゅう
反 5 角 柱
*HAN - GO - KAKU-CHUU*

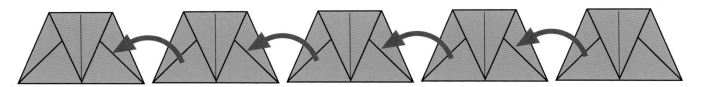

You need 5 Antiprism Modules from page 21.
Insert a flap into the pocket of another module and do
the same three more times. Then tuck the flap into the
pocket at the other end.

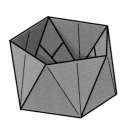

The completed
PENTAGONAL
ANTIPRISM

# HEXAGONAL ANTIPRISM

はん ろっ かく ちゅう
反 6 角 柱
*HAN - ROK - KAKU-CHUU*

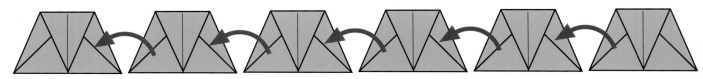

You need 6 Antiprism Modules from page 21.
Insert a flap into the pocket of another module and do
the same four more times. Then tuck the flap into the
pocket at the other end.

The completed
HEXAGONAL
ANTIPRISM

# Arrangements of Antiprisms

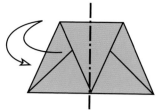

① (This is the Antiprism Module from page 21. You need 3 modules.)
Fold along the center line and unfold. Do the same to the other two modules.

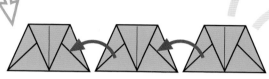

② Insert a flap into the pocket of another module and do the same. Then tuck the flap into the pocket at the other end. You can make two types of models.

Type 1

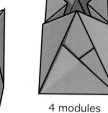

3 modules

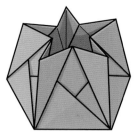

4 modules

5 modules

Type 2

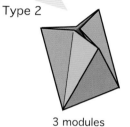

3 modules

4 modules

5 modules

# PYRAMIDS

### TRIANGULAR PYRAMID
 Diagram: Page 25

### SQUARE PYRAMID
 Diagram: Page 26

### PENTAGONAL PYRAMID
Diagram: Page 26

### HEXAGONAL PYRAMID
Diagram: Page 26

# TRIANGULAR PYRAMID

さん かく すい
3 角 錐
SAN - KAKU - SUI

You need 3 square pieces of paper, all the same size.

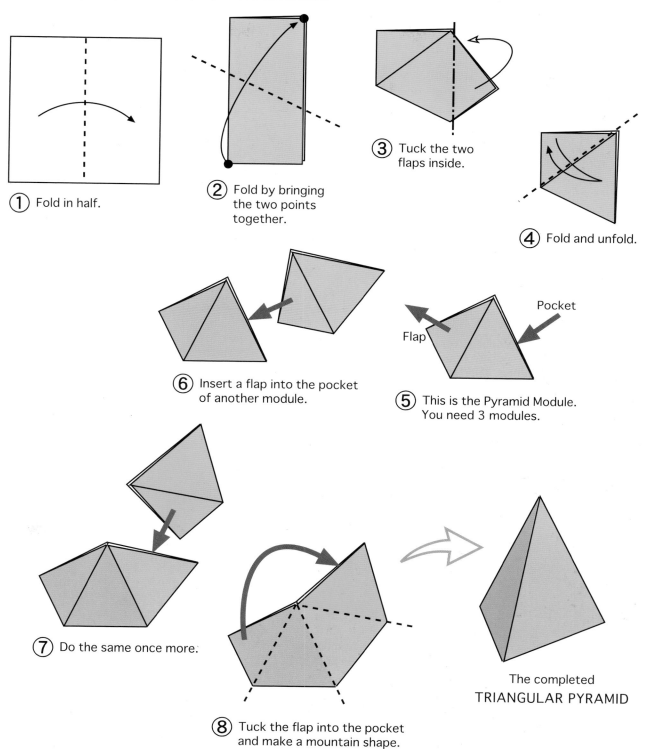

① Fold in half.

② Fold by bringing the two points together.

③ Tuck the two flaps inside.

④ Fold and unfold.

⑥ Insert a flap into the pocket of another module.

Pocket

Flap

⑤ This is the Pyramid Module. You need 3 modules.

⑦ Do the same once more.

⑧ Tuck the flap into the pocket and make a mountain shape.

The completed
TRIANGULAR PYRAMID

# SQUARE PYRAMID

4 角錐
し かく すい
SHI - KAKU - SUI

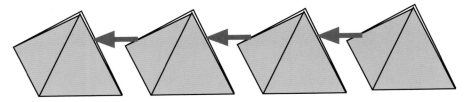

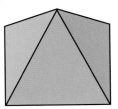

The completed
**SQUARE PYRAMID**

You need 4 Pyramid Modules from page 25.
Insert a flap into the pocket of another module and do the
same two more times. Then tuck the flap into the pocket
at the other end and make a mountain shape.

# PENTAGONAL PYRAMID

5 角錐
ご かく すい
GO - KAKU - SUI

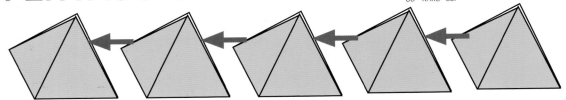

You need 5 Pyramid Modules from page 25.
Insert a flap into the pocket of another module and do the
same three more times. Then tuck the flap into the pocket
at the other end and make a mountain shape.

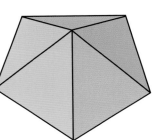

The completed
**PENTAGONAL
PYRAMID**

# HEXAGONAL PYRAMID

6 角錐
ろっ かく すい
ROK - KAKU - SUI

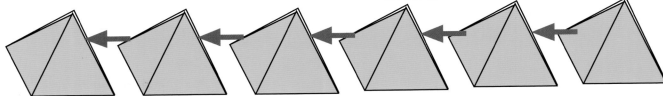

You need 6 Pyramid Modules from page 25.
Insert a flap into the pocket of another module and do the
same four more times. Then tuck the flap into the pocket
at the other end and make a mountain shape.

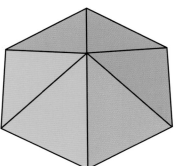

The completed
**HEXAGONAL
PYRAMID**

# DIPYRAMIDS 両角錐
りょう かく すい
*RYOU-KAKU-SUI*

You need 3 square pieces of paper,
all the same size.

Turn the model over

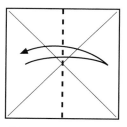

① Fold and unfold.

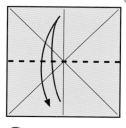

② Fold and unfold.

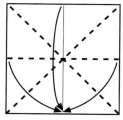

③ Fold and unfold.

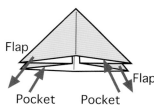

④ Fold by using all the creases at the same time.

⑤ This is the Dipyramid Module. You need 3 modules.

Flap

Flap

Pocket    Pocket

Turn the model over

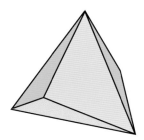

The completed
**DIPYRAMID**

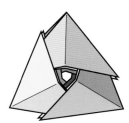

⑧ Pushing gently, bit by bit, bring the pieces together. (The models is no longer flat.)

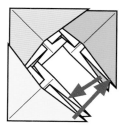

⑦ Push together and insert the last two flaps into the last two pockets.

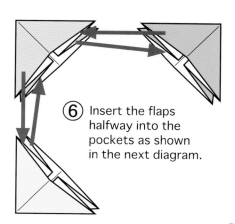

⑥ Insert the flaps halfway into the pockets as shown in the next diagram.

# POLYHEDRON 多面体
*TA - MEN - TAI*

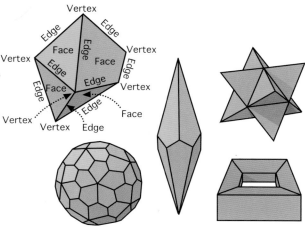

- A polyhedron is a 3-D solid with polygonal faces.
- The names of these shapes come from Greek and Latin words. For example, "tetra" means four, "octa" is eight and "dodeca" is twelve.
- Every polyhedron has vertices, edges and faces enclosing a space. The inside of the polyhedron is called the interior, and the outside is the exterior.

## REGULAR POLYHEDRON 正多面体
*SEI - TA - MEN - TAI*

- A regular polyhedron is a polyhedron whose faces are all identical, regular polygons and whose vertices are formed by the same number of faces. (See "Regular Polygon" on page 99.)
- There are nine kinds of regular polyhedra. Four of them are stellated polyhedra. (See "Star Polyhedra" on page 86.)

★ Tetrahedron
正4面体/せいしめんたい
( *SEI-SHI-MEN-TAI* )

| The shape and number of faces | 4 | Equilateral Triangles | △ |
|---|---|---|---|
| The number of edges and vertices | 6 Edges | 4 Vertices | |

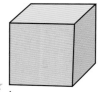

★ Cube
立方体/りっぽうたい
( *RIP-POU-TAI* )

| 6 | Squares | ▢ |
|---|---|---|
| 12 Edges | 8 Vertices | |

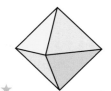

★ Octahedron
正8面体/せいはちめんたい
( *SEI-HACHI-MEN-TAI* )

| 8 | Equilateral Triangles | △ |
|---|---|---|
| 12 Edges | 6 Vertices | |

★ Dodecahedron
正12面体/せいじゅうにめんたい
( *SEI-JUUNI-MEN-TAI* )

| 12 | Regular Pentagons | ⬠ |
|---|---|---|
| 30 Edges | 20 Vertices | |

★ Icosahedron
正20面体/せいにじゅうめんたい
( *SEI-NIJUU-MEN-TAI* )

| 20 | Equilateral Triangles | △ |
|---|---|---|
| 30 Edges | 12 Vertices | |

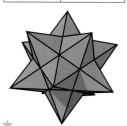

★ Small Stellated Dodecahedron
小星形12面体/しょうほしがたじゅうにめんたい
( *SHOU-HOSI-GATA-JUUNI-MEN-TAI* )

| 12 | Regular Stellated Pentagons | ✪ |
|---|---|---|
| 30 Edges | 20 Vertices | |

★ Great Dodecahedron
大12面体/だいじゅうにめんたい
( *DAI-JUUNI-MEN-TAI* )

| 12 | Regular Pentagons | ⬠ |
|---|---|---|
| 30 Edges | 20 Vertices | |

★ Great Stellated Dodecahedron
大星形12面体/だいほしがたじゅうにめんたい
( *DAI-HOSHI-GATA-JUUNI-MEN-TAI* )

| 12 | Regular Stellated Pentagons | ★ |
|---|---|---|
| 30 Edges | 20 Vertices | |

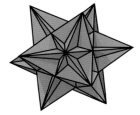

★ Great Icosahedron
大20面体/だいにじゅうめんたい
( *DAI-NIJUU-MEN-TAI* )

| 20 | Equilateral Triangules | △ |
|---|---|---|
| 30 Edges | 12 Vertices | |

- There are three groups of regular and semi-regular polyhedra:
  ★ The regular tetrahedron group   ★ The cube and regular octahedron group
  ★ The regular dodecahedron and regular icosahedron group

# SEMI-REGULAR POLYHEDRON

準正多面体 (じゅん せい た めんたい)
JUN - SEI - TA - MEN - TAI

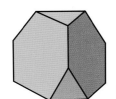

### Truncated Tetrahedron
切頂4面体/せっちょうしめんたい
( SET-CHOU-SHI-MEN-TAI )

| The shapes and the number of faces | 4 | Equilateral Triangules | |
|---|---|---|---|
| | 4 | Regular Hexagons | |
| The number of edges and vertices | 18 Edges | 12 Vertices | |

- A semi-regular polyhedron is made up of two or three kinds of regular polygonal faces with all vertices having the same structure.
- There are 13 kinds of semi-regular polyhedra. (There are 53 kinds of semi-regular stellated polyhedra.)

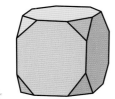

### Truncated Cube
切頂立方体/せっちょうりっぽうたい
( SET-CHOU-RIP-POU-TAI )

| 8 | Equilateral Triangules | |
|---|---|---|
| 6 | Regular Octagons | |
| 36 Edges | 24 Vertices | |

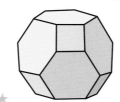

### Truncated Octahedron
切頂8面体/せっちょうはちめんたい
( SET-CHOU-HACHI-MEN-TAI )

| 6 | Squares | |
|---|---|---|
| 8 | Regular Hexagons | |
| 36 Edges | 24 Vertices | |

### Truncated Dodecahedron
切頂12面体/せっちょうじゅうにめんたい
( SET-CHOU-JUUNI-MEN-TAI )

| 20 | Equilateral Triangules | |
|---|---|---|
| 12 | Regular Decagons | |
| 90 Edges | 60 Vertices | |

### Truncated Icosahedron
切頂20面体/せっちょうにじゅうめんたい
( SET-CHOU-NIJUU-MEN-TAI )

| 12 | Regular Pentagons | |
|---|---|---|
| 20 | Regular Hexagons | |
| 90 Edges | 60 Vertices | |

### Cuboctahedron
立方8面体/りっぽうはちめんたい
( RIP-POU-HACHI-MEN-TAI )

| 8 | Equilateral Triangules | |
|---|---|---|
| 6 | Squares | |
| 24 Edges | 12 Vertices | |

### Icosidodecahedron
20・12面体/にじゅうじゅうにめんたい
( NIJUU-JUUNI-MEN-TAI )

| 20 | Equilateral Triangules | |
|---|---|---|
| 12 | Regular Pentagons | |
| 60 Edges | 30 Vertices | |

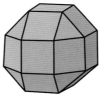

### Rombicuboctahedron
斜方立方8面体/しゃほうりっぽうはちめんたい
( SHA-HOU-RIP-POU-HACHI-MEN-TAI )

| 8 | Equilateral Triangules | |
|---|---|---|
| 18 | Squares | |
| 48 Edges | 24 Vertices | |

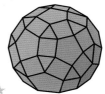

### Rhombicosi-dodecahedron
斜方20・12面体
/しゃほうにじゅうじゅうにめんたい
( SHA-HOU-NIJUU-JUUNI-MEN-TAI )

| 20 | Equilateral Triangules | |
|---|---|---|
| 30 | Squares | |
| 12 | Regular Pentagons | |
| 120 Edges | 60 Vertices | |

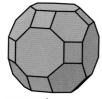

### Truncated Cuboctahedron
斜方切頂立方8面体
/しゃほうせっちょうりっぽうはちめんたい
( SHA-HOU-SET-CHOU-RIP-POU-HACHI-MEN-TAI )

| 12 | Squares | |
|---|---|---|
| 8 | Regular Hexagons | |
| 6 | Regular Octagons | |
| 72 Edges | 48 Vertices | |

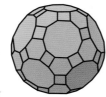

### Truncated Icosidodecahedron
斜方切頂20・12面体
/しゃほうせっちょうにじゅうじゅうにめんたい
( SHA-HOU-SET-CHOU-NIJUU-JUUNI-MEN-TAI )

| 30 | Squares | |
|---|---|---|
| 20 | Regular Hexagons | |
| 12 | Regular Octagons | |
| 180 Edges | 120 Vertices | |

### Snub Cube
変形立方体/へんけいりっぽうたい
( HEN-KEI-RIP-POU-TAI )

| 32 | Equilateral Triangules | |
|---|---|---|
| 6 | Squares | |
| 60 Edges | 24 Vertices | |

### Snub Dodecahedron
変形12面体/へんけいじゅうにめんたい
( HEN-KEI-JUUNI-MEN-TAI )

| 80 | Equilateral Triangules | |
|---|---|---|
| 12 | Regular Pentagons | |
| 150 Edges | 60 Vertices | |

# REGULAR POLYHEDRA

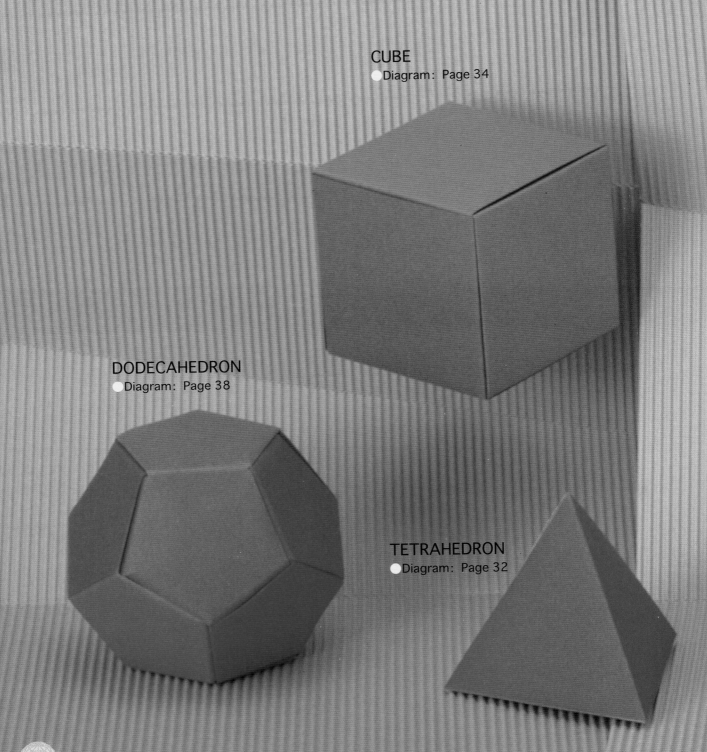

CUBE
● Diagram: Page 34

DODECAHEDRON
● Diagram: Page 38

TETRAHEDRON
● Diagram: Page 32

## ICOSAHEDRON
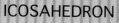Diagram: Page 40

## OCTAHEDRON
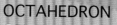Diagram: Page 36

# TETRAHEDRON
せい し めん たい
正 4 面 体
*SEI - SHI - MEN - TAI*

You need 2 square pieces of paper, both the same size.

① Fold in half and unfold.

② Bring the lower left corner to the center line and fold. Make sure the fold goes through the lower right corner.

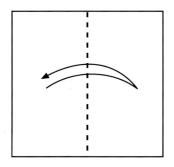

③ Bring the two points marked ● together and fold.

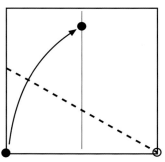

④ Fold along the edge.

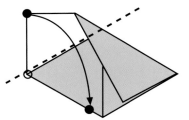

⑤ Fold along the edge.

⑥ You need 2 identical pieces. Unfold both back to a square.

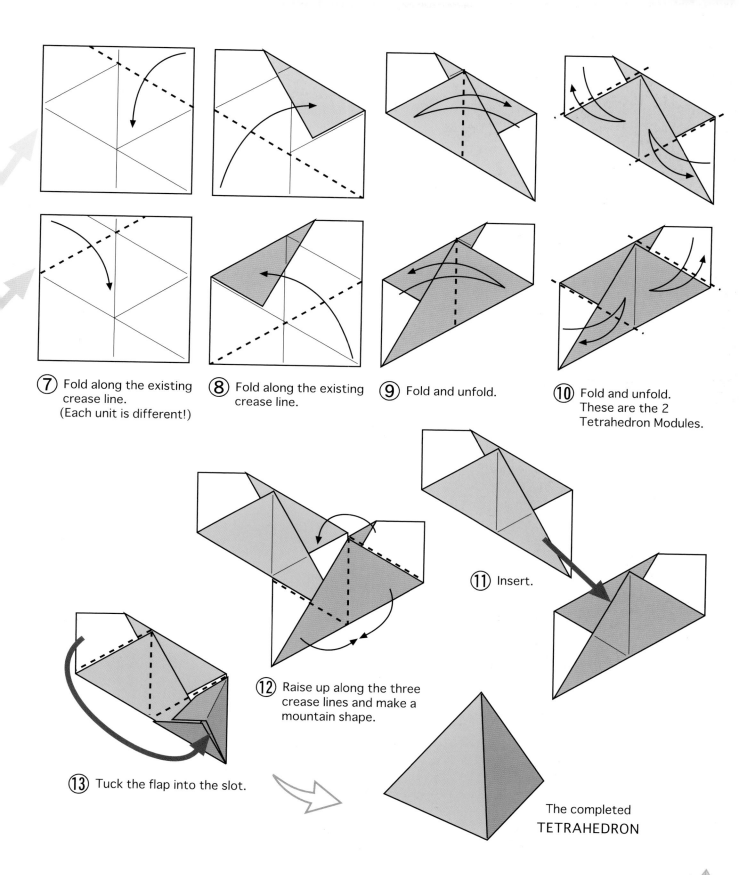

⑦ Fold along the existing crease line. (Each unit is different!)

⑧ Fold along the existing crease line.

⑨ Fold and unfold.

⑩ Fold and unfold. These are the 2 Tetrahedron Modules.

⑪ Insert.

⑫ Raise up along the three crease lines and make a mountain shape.

⑬ Tuck the flap into the slot.

The completed TETRAHEDRON

# CUBE 立方体
りっ ぼう たい
*RIP - POU - TAI*

● This "Cube" is a slightly different arrangment of the "Cube" by Paul Jackson.

You need 6 square pieces of paper,
all the same size.

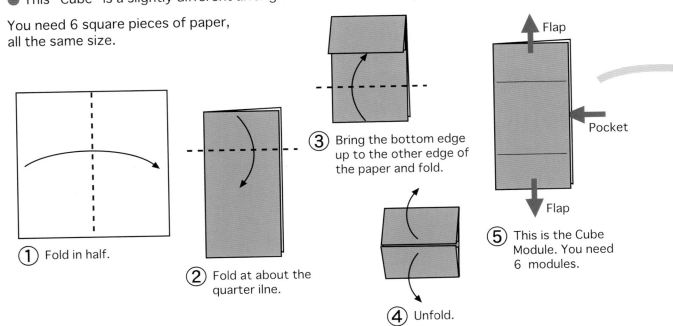

① Fold in half.

② Fold at about the quarter ilne.

③ Bring the bottom edge up to the other edge of the paper and fold.

④ Unfold.

Flap

Pocket

Flap

⑤ This is the Cube Module. You need 6 modules.

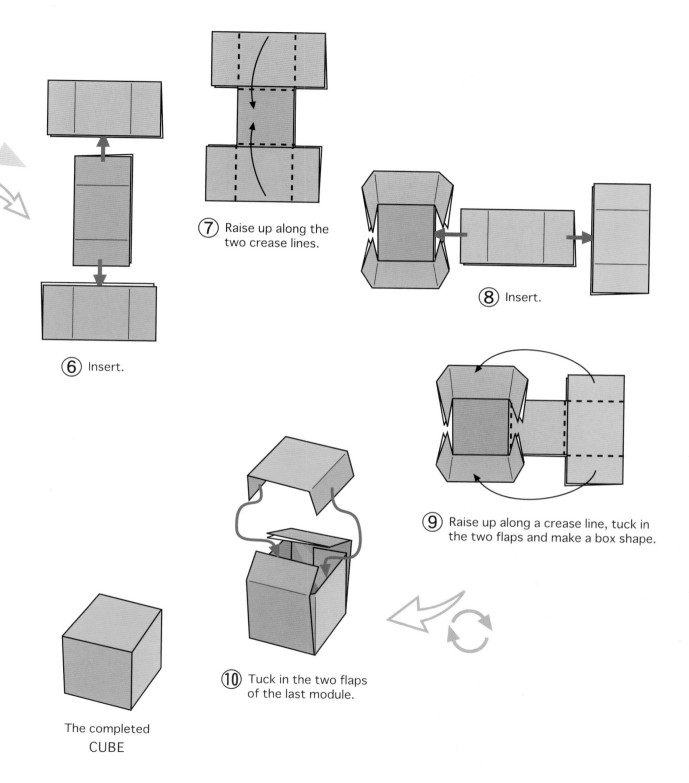

⑥ Insert.

⑦ Raise up along the two crease lines.

⑧ Insert.

⑨ Raise up along a crease line, tuck in the two flaps and make a box shape.

⑩ Tuck in the two flaps of the last module.

The completed
CUBE

# OCTAHEDRON

正 8 面体
せい はち めん たい
SEI - HACHI-MEN - TAI

You need 4 square pieces of paper, all the same size.

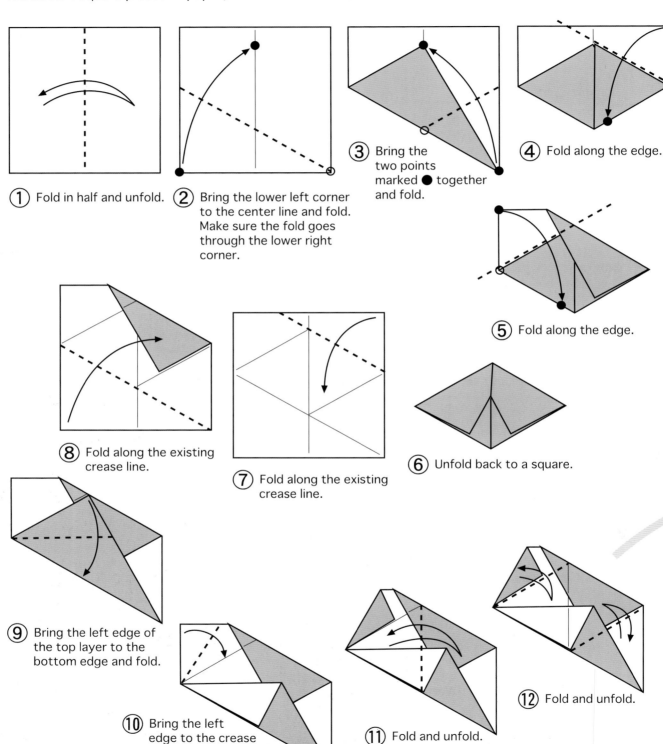

① Fold in half and unfold.

② Bring the lower left corner to the center line and fold. Make sure the fold goes through the lower right corner.

③ Bring the two points marked ● together and fold.

④ Fold along the edge.

⑤ Fold along the edge.

⑥ Unfold back to a square.

⑦ Fold along the existing crease line.

⑧ Fold along the existing crease line.

⑨ Bring the left edge of the top layer to the bottom edge and fold.

⑩ Bring the left edge to the crease line and fold.

⑪ Fold and unfold.

⑫ Fold and unfold.

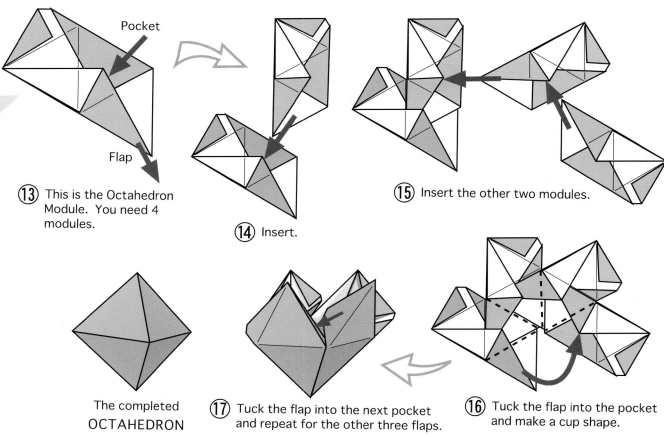

**Pocket**

**Flap**

⑬ This is the Octahedron Module. You need 4 modules.

⑭ Insert.

⑮ Insert the other two modules.

The completed
**OCTAHEDRON**

⑰ Tuck the flap into the next pocket and repeat for the other three flaps.

⑯ Tuck the flap into the pocket and make a cup shape.

# DODECAHEDRON

せい じゅうに めん たい
正 12 面 体
SEI - JUUNI - MEN - TAI

You need 12 square pieces of paper,
all the same size.

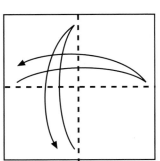

① Fold and unfold.
Do the same in the
other direction.

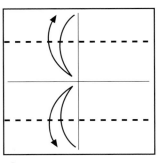

② Fold the bottom edge
up to the center line
and fold. Do the same
with the upper edge.

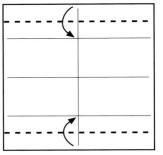

③ Fold the bottom edge
up to the quarter line
and fold. Do the same
with the upper edge.

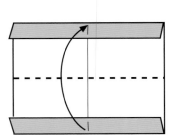

④ Fold the bottom edge
up to the top.

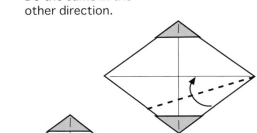

⑦ Bring the lower right
edge up to the center
line and fold.

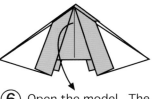

⑥ Open the model. The
lower corners will overlap
on the back.

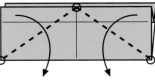

⑤ Fold just the upper layer
in front. Do the same on
the reverse side.

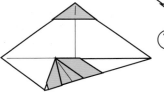

⑧ Unfold back to a square.

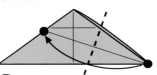

⑬ Bring the two points
marked ● together
and fold.

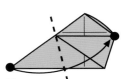

⑭ Bring the two points
marked ● together
and fold.

In process
(Top view)

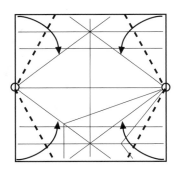

⑨ Bring the four edges to
each of the crease lines.

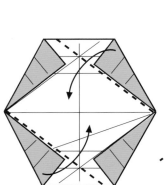

⑩ Fold along the two
crease lines.

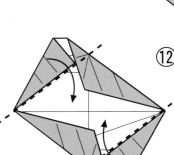

⑪ Fold along the two crease lines.

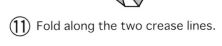

⑫ Fold in half and
interlock the flaps.

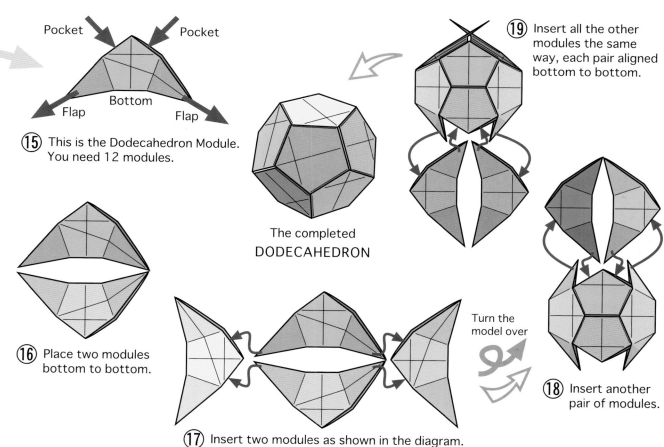

Pocket    Pocket

Bottom
Flap          Flap

⑮ This is the Dodecahedron Module. You need 12 modules.

⑯ Place two modules bottom to bottom.

⑰ Insert two modules as shown in the diagram.

The completed
**DODECAHEDRON**

⑲ Insert all the other modules the same way, each pair aligned bottom to bottom.

Turn the model over

⑱ Insert another pair of modules.

# ICOSAHEDRON 正 20 面体

せい にじゅう めん たい
SEI - NIJUU - MEN - TAI

You need 10 square pieces of paper, all the same size.

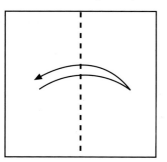

① Fold in half and unfold.

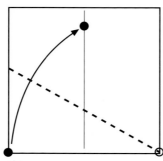

② Bring the lower left corner to the center line and fold. Make sure the fold goes through the lower right corner.

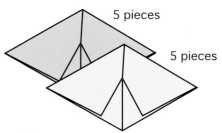

5 pieces

5 pieces

⑥ You need 10 identical pieces. Unfold all of them back to a square.

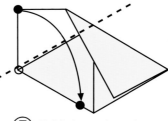

⑤ Fold along the edge.

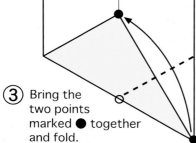

③ Bring the two points marked ● together and fold.

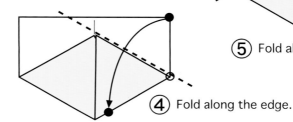

④ Fold along the edge.

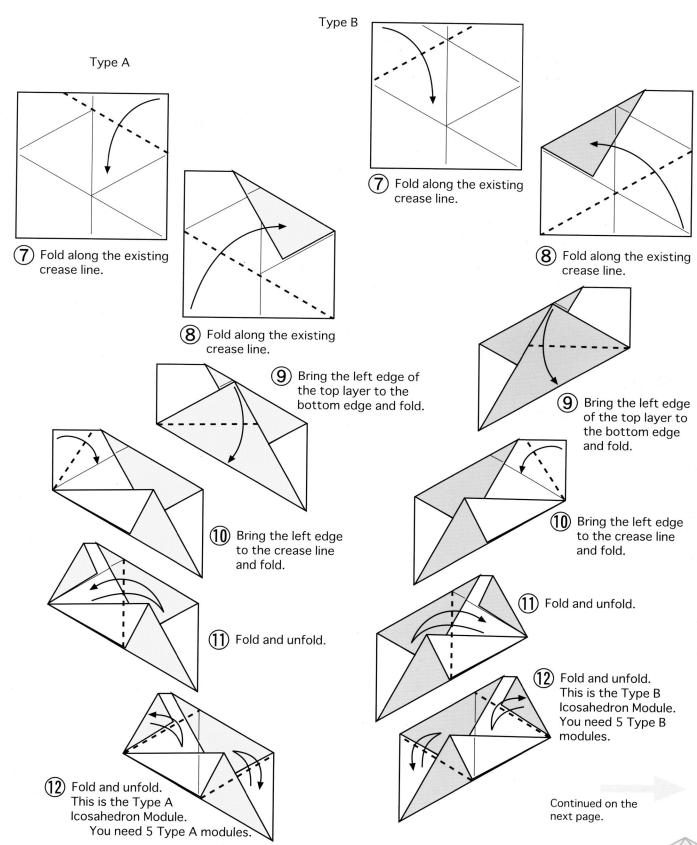

Type A

⑦ Fold along the existing crease line.

⑧ Fold along the existing crease line.

⑨ Bring the left edge of the top layer to the bottom edge and fold.

⑩ Bring the left edge to the crease line and fold.

⑪ Fold and unfold.

⑫ Fold and unfold. This is the Type A Icosahedron Module. You need 5 Type A modules.

Type B

⑦ Fold along the existing crease line.

⑧ Fold along the existing crease line.

⑨ Bring the left edge of the top layer to the bottom edge and fold.

⑩ Bring the left edge to the crease line and fold.

⑪ Fold and unfold.

⑫ Fold and unfold. This is the Type B Icosahedron Module. You need 5 Type B modules.

Continued on the next page.

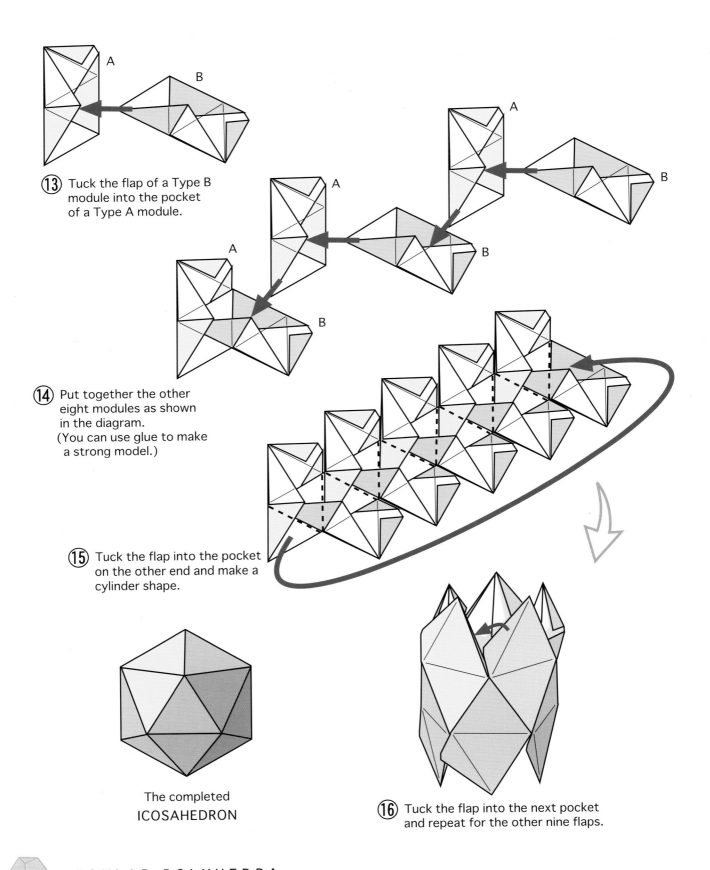

⑬ Tuck the flap of a Type B module into the pocket of a Type A module.

⑭ Put together the other eight modules as shown in the diagram. (You can use glue to make a strong model.)

⑮ Tuck the flap into the pocket on the other end and make a cylinder shape.

The completed
ICOSAHEDRON

⑯ Tuck the flap into the next pocket and repeat for the other nine flaps.

# PAPER BALLOON

紙風船
KAMI - FUU - SEN

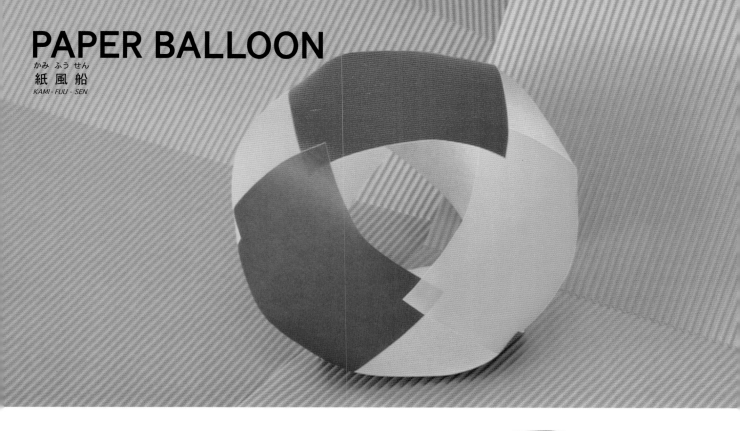

You need 6 square pieces of paper, all the same size.

① Glue five sheets of
square paper as shown
in the diagram.

② Glue on another one.

③ Put together the corners and
glue as shown in the diagram.

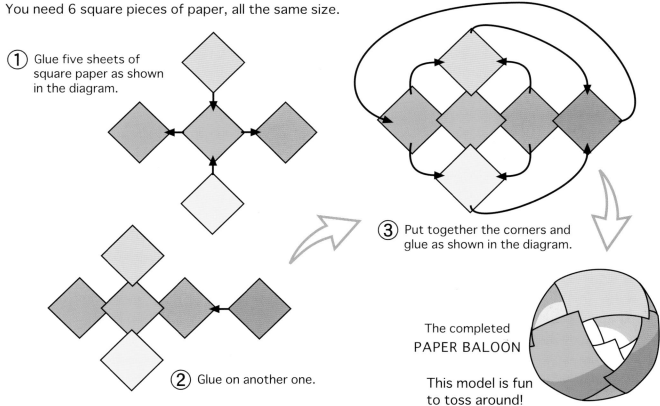

The completed
PAPER BALOON

This model is fun
to toss around!

# POLYHEDRAL SKELETONS

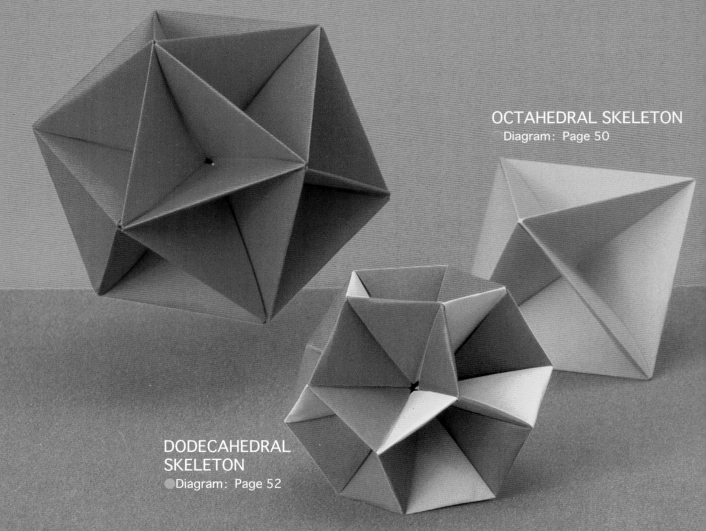

ICOSAHEDRAL SKELETON
○Diagram: Page 54

OCTAHEDRAL SKELETON
○Diagram: Page 50

DODECAHEDRAL
SKELETON
●Diagram: Page 52

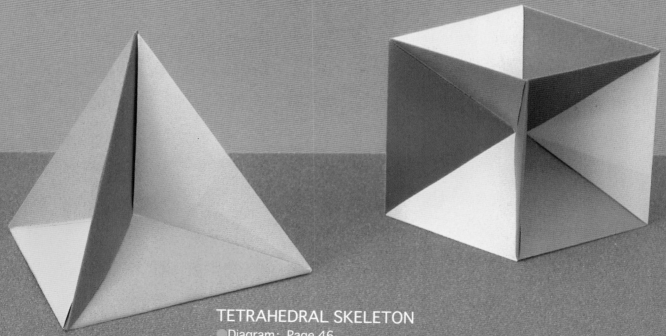

**CUBE SKELETON**
Diagram: Page 48

**TETRAHEDRAL SKELETON**
Diagram: Page 46

# TETRAHEDRAL SKELETON

せい し めんたい　　すけ る と ん
正4面体のスケルトン
SEI - SHI - MEN - TAI　NO　SU - KE - RU - TO - N

You need 6 square pieces of paper, all the same size.

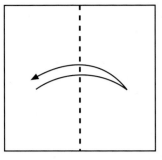

① Fold in half and unfold.

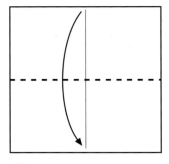

② Fold in half.

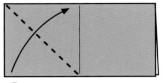

③ Fold only one layer, bringing the left edge to the top edge.

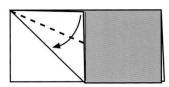

④ Fold only one layer, bringing the top edge to the slanted edge.

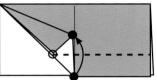

⑤ Bring the two points marked ● together and fold only one layer.

Turn the model over

⑦ Fold only one layer along the crease line.

⑥ Unfold back to step ③.

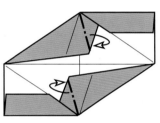

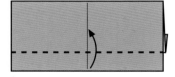

⑧ Fold along the edge of the reverse side.

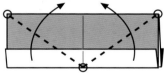

⑨ Fold only one layer.

Turn the model over

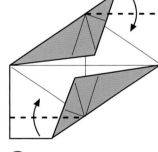

⑭ Fold along the two crease lines.

⑮ Tuck the two small triangles under the top layer and pull out the two hidden parts as shown in the next diagram.

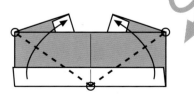

⑩ Do the same on the reverse side.

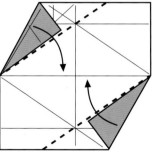

⑬ Fold along the two crease lines.

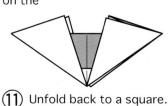

⑪ Unfold back to a square.

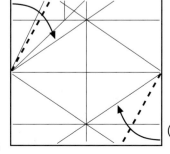

⑫ Fold by bringing the left edge to the slanted crease line. Do the same on the right edge.

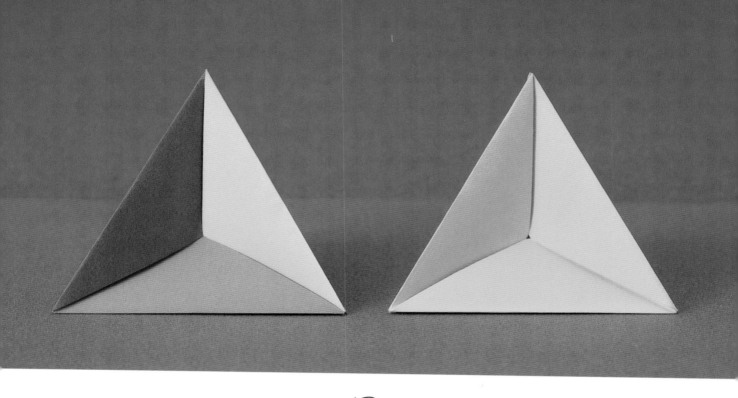

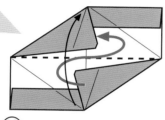

⑯ Fold in half and interlock the flaps.

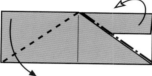

⑰ Fold along the edges.

⑱ Fold a little above the bottom edge. Do the same on the reverse side.

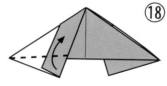

Pocket   Pocket

Flap                    Flap

⑲ This is the Tetrahedral Skeleton Module. You need 6 modules.

㉑

⑳ Insert the flaps into the pockets all around and make a dish shape.

Turn the model over

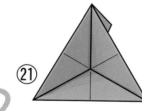

This corner is formed by 3 modules.

This interior corner is also formed by 3 modules.

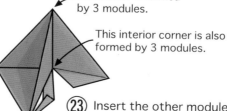

㉒ Insert the flap on the new piece into the pocket on the dish shape. Then insert the flap on the dish shape into the pocket on the new piece.

㉓ Insert the other modules the same way.

The completed
TETRAHEDRAL
SKELETON

# CUBE SKELETON

立方体のスケルトン
RIP - POU - TAI  NO  SU - KE - RU - TO - N

You need 12 square pieces of paper, all the same size.

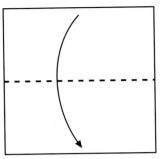

① Fold in half.

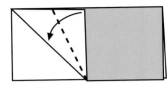

② Fold only one layer, bringing the left edge to the top edge.

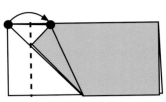

③ Fold only one layer, bringing the right edge to the slanted edge.

④ Bring the two points marked ● together and fold.

⑤ Turn the model over.

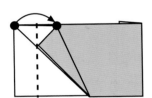

⑧ Bring the two points marked ● together and fold.

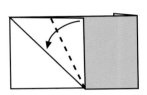

⑦ Fold only one layer, bringing the right edge to the slanted edge.

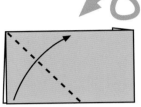

⑥ Fold only one layer, bringing the left edge to the top edge.

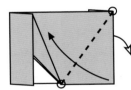

⑨ Fold the corner up and to the left as shown. Allow the flap at the back to swing out to the right.

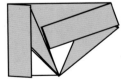

⑩ Turn the model over.

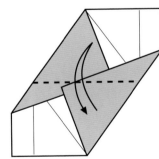

⑭ Fold and unfold.

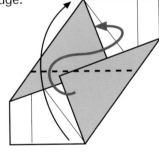

⑮ Fold in half and interlock the flaps.

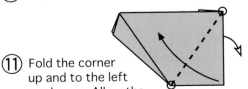

⑪ Fold the corner up and to the left as shown. Allow the flap at the back to swing out to the right.

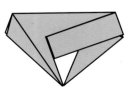

⑫ Unfold back to a square.

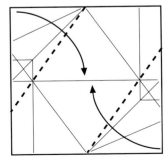

⑬ Fold along the two crease lines.

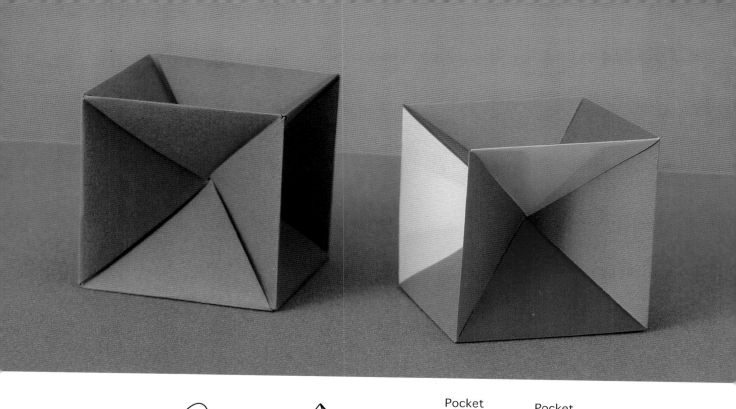

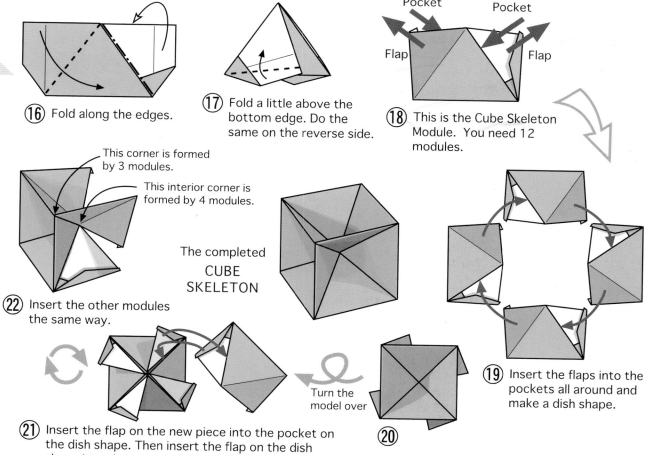

⑯ Fold along the edges.

⑰ Fold a little above the bottom edge. Do the same on the reverse side.

Pocket    Pocket

Flap        Flap

⑱ This is the Cube Skeleton Module. You need 12 modules.

This corner is formed by 3 modules.

This interior corner is formed by 4 modules.

The completed
CUBE
SKELETON

㉒ Insert the other modules the same way.

⑲ Insert the flaps into the pockets all around and make a dish shape.

Turn the model over

⑳

㉑ Insert the flap on the new piece into the pocket on the dish shape. Then insert the flap on the dish shape into the pocket on the new piece.

# OCTAHEDRAL SKELETON

正 8 面体のスケルトン
SEI-HACHI-MEN-TAI NO SU-KE-RU-TO-N

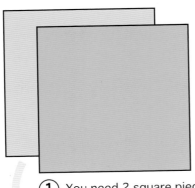

① You need 2 square pieces of paper, both the same size.

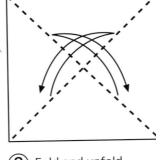

② Fold and unfold.

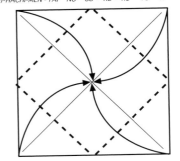

③ Bring each corner to the center point and fold.

② Fold and unfold.

③ Cut the paper along the crease lines.

④ You need 1 small piece of paper.

⑤ Fold and unfold.

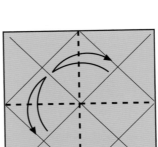

④ Unfold back to a square.

Turn the model over

⑤ Fold and unfold.

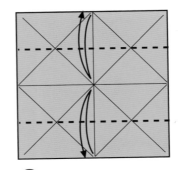

⑥ Fold and unfold.

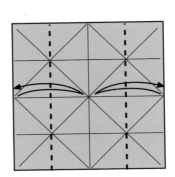

⑦ Fold and unfold.

Turn the model over

⑥ Fold and unfold.

⑦ Fold by using all the creases at the same time.

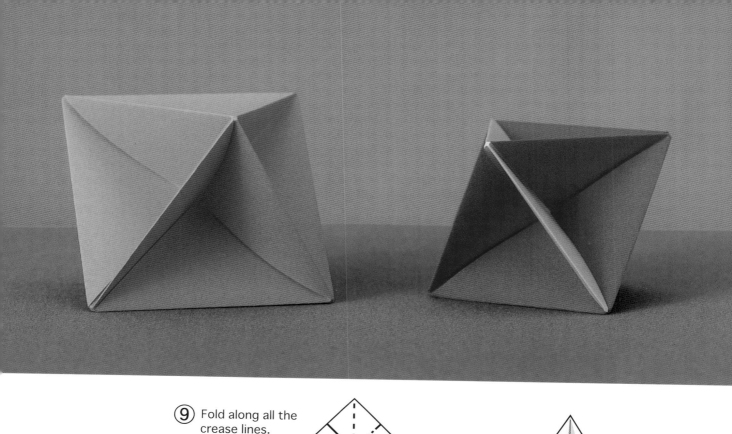

⑨ Fold along all the crease lines. The model will become 3-D.

Turn the model over

⑩ Tuck the four points into the inside as shown in the diagram.

⑧ Cut.

⑧ This is the cap.

⑪ Tuck the two points of the cap marked ◎ inside two points of the lower piece. Do the opposite with the other cap points.

The completed
**OCTAHEDRAL SKELETON**

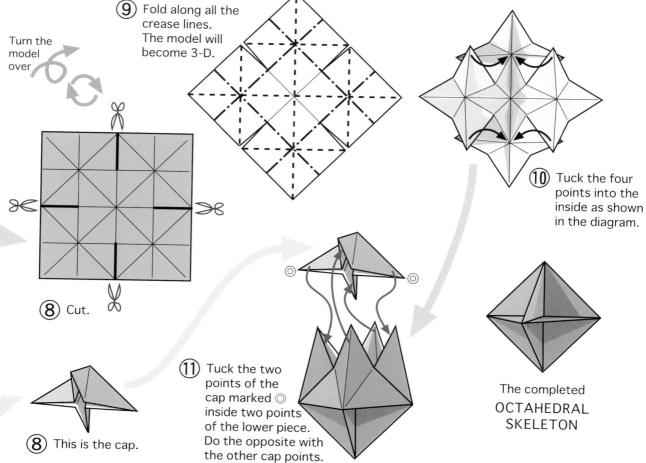

# DODECAHEDRAL SKELETON

せいじゅうにめんたい　　すけるとん
正 12 面体 の スケルトン
SEI - JUUNI - MEN - TAI　NO　SU - KE - RU - TO - N

You need 30 square pieces of paper, all the same size.

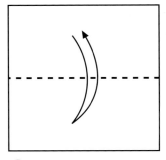

① Fold in half and unfold.

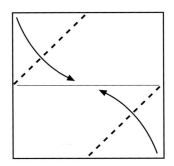

② Bring the lower right edge to the center line and fold. Do the same on the upper side.

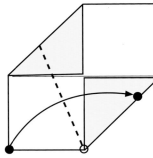

③ Bring the bottom edge to the right slanted edge and fold.

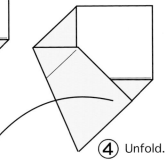

④ Unfold.

⑦ Bring the lower right corner to a point a little inside the crease and fold. Do the same on the upper left corner.

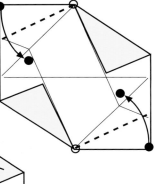

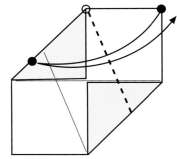

⑤ Bring the top edge to the left slanted edge and fold. Then unfold back to a square.

⑥ Bring the bottom edge to the crease and fold. Do the same on the top edge.

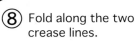

⑧ Fold along the two crease lines.

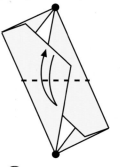

⑨ Fold by bringing the two points together and unfold.

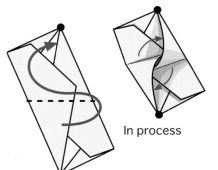

In process

⑩ Fold in half and interlock the flaps.

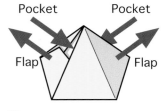

Pocket      Pocket

Flap          Flap

⑫ This is the Dodecahedral Skeleton Module. You need 30 modules.

⑪ Fold and unfold.

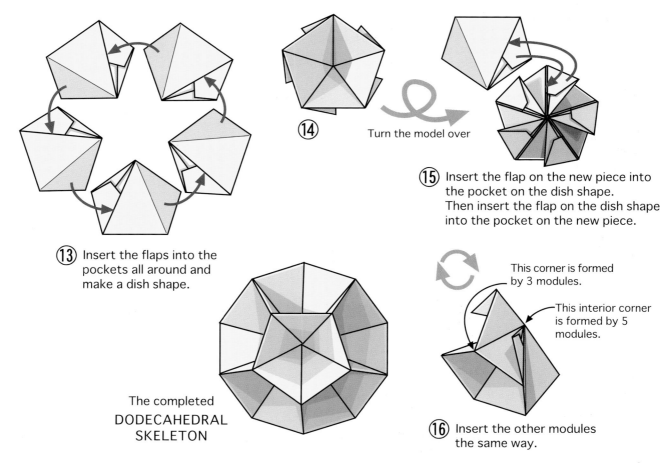

⑬ Insert the flaps into the pockets all around and make a dish shape.

⑭

Turn the model over

⑮ Insert the flap on the new piece into the pocket on the dish shape.
Then insert the flap on the dish shape into the pocket on the new piece.

This corner is formed by 3 modules.

This interior corner is formed by 5 modules.

⑯ Insert the other modules the same way.

The completed
**DODECAHEDRAL SKELETON**

# ICOSAHEDRAL SKELETON

You need 30 square pieces of paper, all the same size.

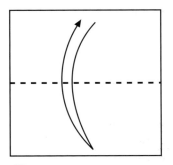

① Fold in half and unfold.

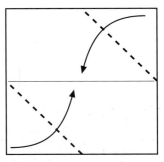

② Bring the lower right edge to the center line and fold. Do the same on the upper side.

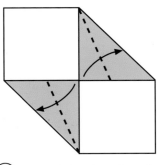

③ Bring the right edge of the lower triangle to the left edge and fold. Do the same on the upper side.

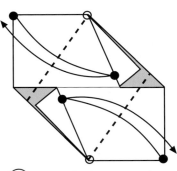

④ Bring the bottom edge to the left inside edge and fold. Do the same on the top edge and then unfold back to a square.

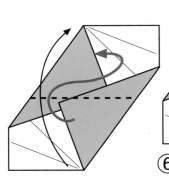

⑦ Fold in half and interlock the flaps.

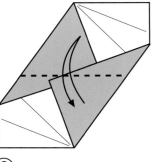

⑥ Fold and unfold.

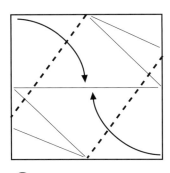

⑤ Fold along the two crease lines.

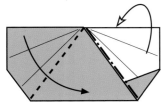

⑧ Fold along the edges.

⑨ Fold a little above the bottom edge. Do the same on the reverse side.

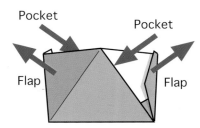

Pocket    Pocket

Flap    Flap

⑩ This is the Icosahedral Skeleton Module. You need 30 modules.

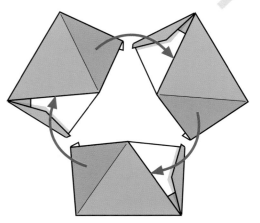

⑪ Insert the flaps into the pockets all around and make a dish shape.

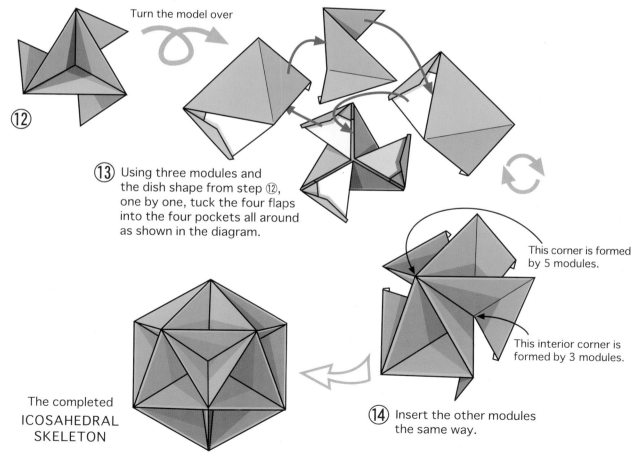

Turn the model over

⑫

⑬ Using three modules and
the dish shape from step ⑫,
one by one, tuck the four flaps
into the four pockets all around
as shown in the diagram.

This corner is formed
by 5 modules.

This interior corner is
formed by 3 modules.

⑭ Insert the other modules
the same way.

The completed
ICOSAHEDRAL
SKELETON

# POLYHEDRAL FRAMES

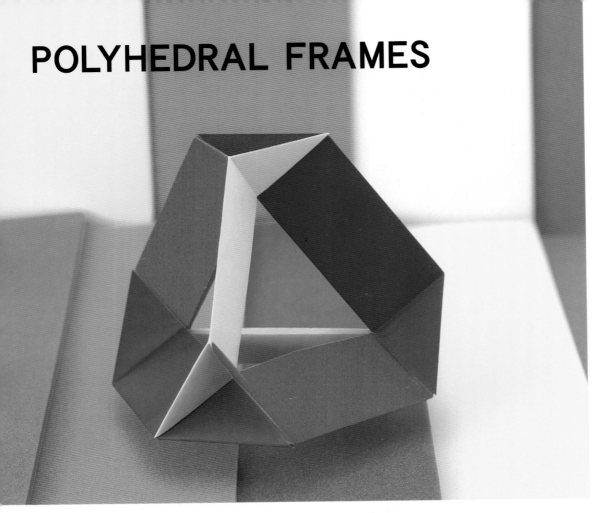

## TRUNCATED TETRAHEDRAL FRAME

しめんたい ふ れ ー む
**4面体のフレーム**
SHI-MEN-TAI NO FU - RE - E - MU

You need 6 square pieces of paper, all the same size.

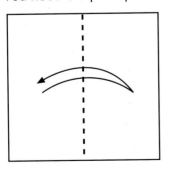

① Fold in half and unfold.

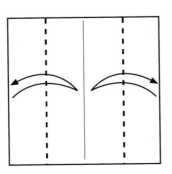

② Fold by bringing the right edge to the center line and unfold. Do the same on the left side.

③ Fold the four corners.

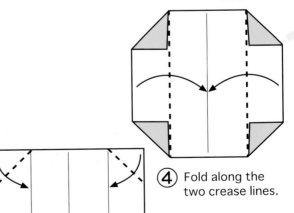

④ Fold along the two crease lines.

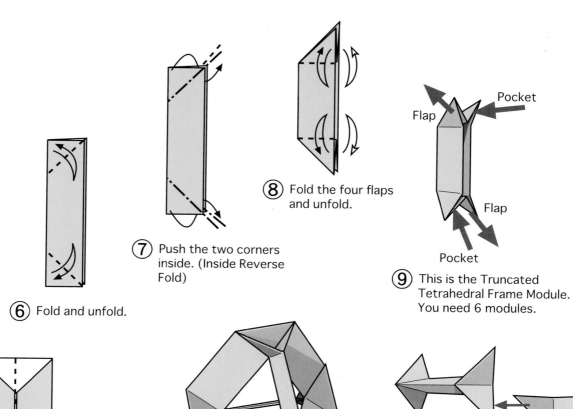

⑧ Fold the four flaps and unfold.

Pocket

Flap

Flap

Pocket

⑦ Push the two corners inside. (Inside Reverse Fold)

⑥ Fold and unfold.

⑨ This is the Truncated Tetrahedral Frame Module. You need 6 modules.

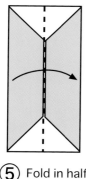

⑤ Fold in half.

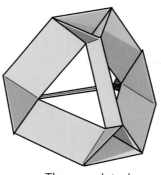

The completed
**TRUNCATED TETRAHEDRAL FRAME**

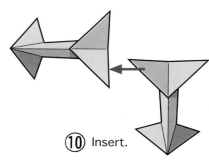

⑩ Insert.

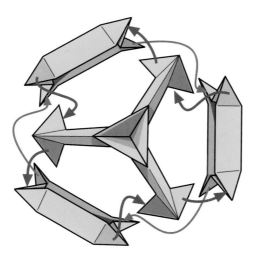

⑫ Put together the other three modules as shown in the diagram.

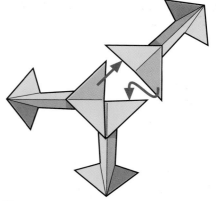

⑪ Insert the two flaps into the two pockets and make a dish shape on the top of the model.

# OCTAHEDRAL FRAME

せいはちめんたい　ふ れ ー む
正 8 面体のフレーム
SEI-HACHI-MEN-TAI  NO  FU - RE - E - MU

You need 6 square pieces of paper, all the same size.

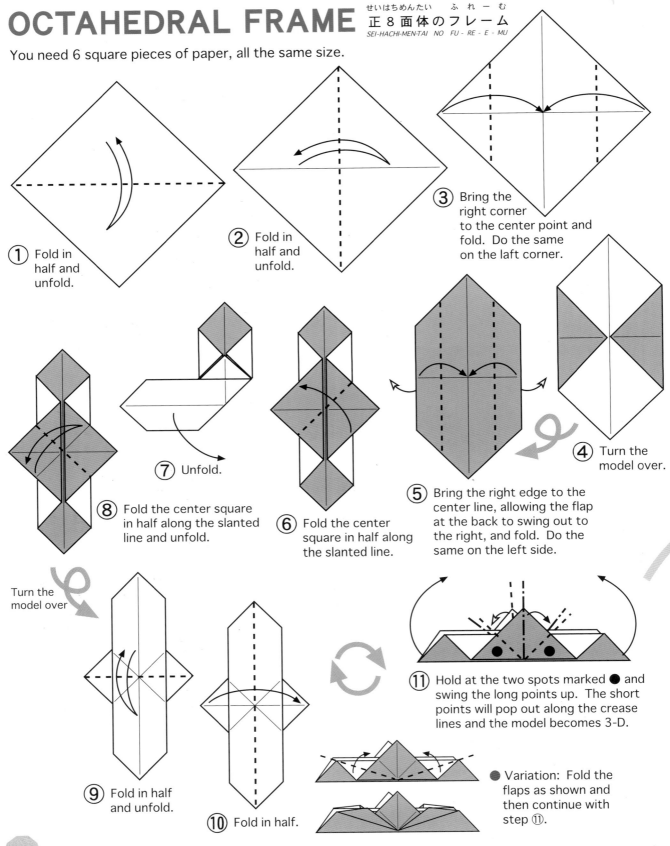

① Fold in half and unfold.

② Fold in half and unfold.

③ Bring the right corner to the center point and fold. Do the same on the laft corner.

④ Turn the model over.

⑤ Bring the right edge to the center line, allowing the flap at the back to swing out to the right, and fold. Do the same on the left side.

⑥ Fold the center square in half along the slanted line.

⑦ Unfold.

⑧ Fold the center square in half along the slanted line and unfold.

Turn the model over

⑨ Fold in half and unfold.

⑩ Fold in half.

⑪ Hold at the two spots marked ● and swing the long points up. The short points will pop out along the crease lines and the model becomes 3-D.

● Variation: Fold the flaps as shown and then continue with step ⑪.

58  POLYHEDRAL FRAMES

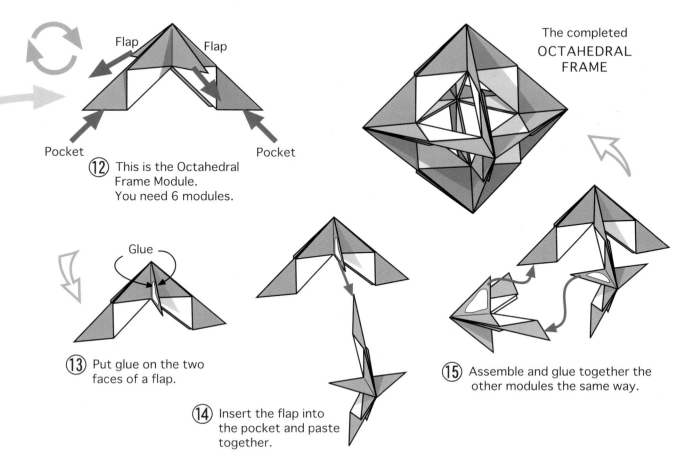

Flap    Flap

Pocket    Pocket

⑫ This is the Octahedral
Frame Module.
You need 6 modules.

The completed
**OCTAHEDRAL
FRAME**

Glue

⑬ Put glue on the two
faces of a flap.

⑭ Insert the flap into
the pocket and paste
together.

⑮ Assemble and glue together the
other modules the same way.

POLYHEDRAL FRAMES  59

# POLYHEDRA KIT

**OCTAHEDRON**
● Diagram: Page 66

**ICOSAHEDRON**
● Diagram: Page 70

**CUBE**
● Diagram: Page 63

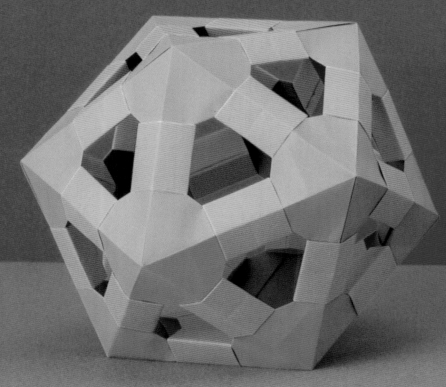

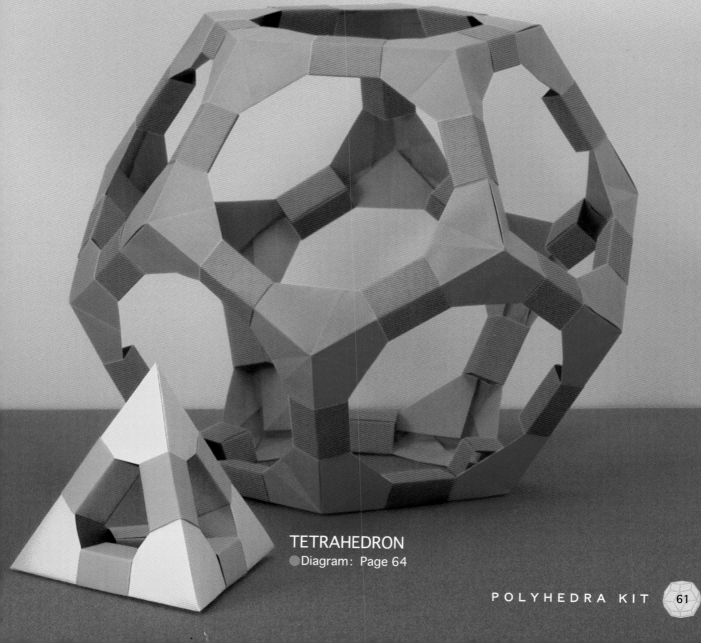

DODECAHEDRON
●Diagram: Page 68

TETRAHEDRON
●Diagram: Page 64

POLYHEDRA KIT    61

# POLYHEDRA KIT: EDGE MODULE

Start with a square piece of paper.

① Fold in half and unfold.

② Fold in half and unfold.

③ Fold by bringing the bottom corner to the center point and unfold. Do the same on the top corner.

④ Bring the bottom corner to the intersection of the center line and the quarter line and fold. Do the same on the top corner.

⑤ Fold along the two crease lines.

Turn the model over

⑥ Bring the right corner to the center point and fold.

⑦ Bring the bottom edge to the center line and fold. Do the same on the top edge.

⑧ Fold and unfold.

⑨ Fold and unfold.

⑩ Fold and unfold.

⑪ Fold and unfold.

⑫ Fold the left corner.

⑬ Tuck the flap into the pocket at the other end.

Pocket

The completed Edge Module

Pocket

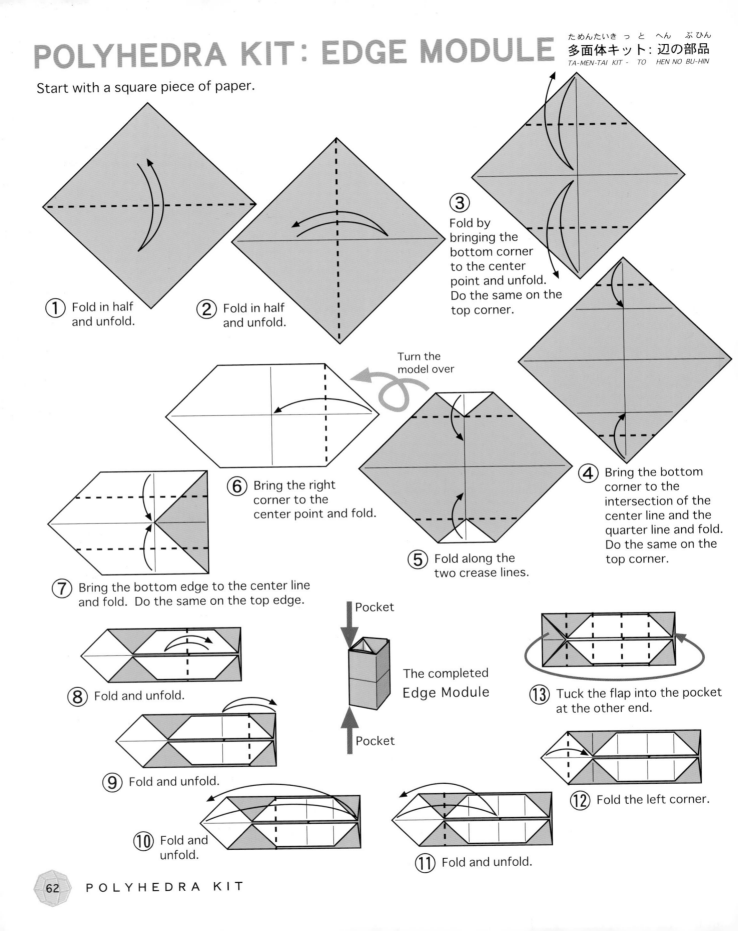

# POLYHEDRA KIT: CUBE 立方体

りっ ぼう たい
*RIP - POU - TAI*

You need 8 RIGHT CORNER 2 units on page 14
and 12 Edge Modules on page 62.
(So you need 20 square pieces of paper, all the same size.)

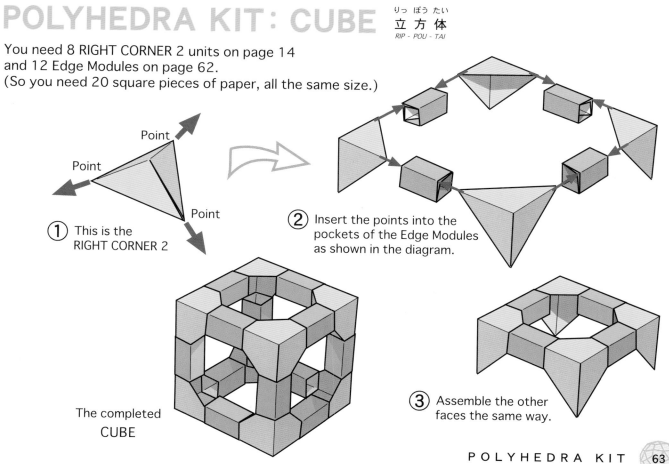

Point

Point

Point

① This is the
RIGHT CORNER 2

② Insert the points into the
pockets of the Edge Modules
as shown in the diagram.

The completed
CUBE

③ Assemble the other
faces the same way.

せい　し　めん　たい
正 4 面 体
*SEI - SHI - MEN - TAI*

You need 10 of the same size, square pieces of paper.

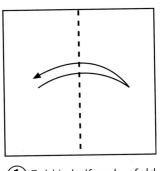

① Fold in half and unfold.

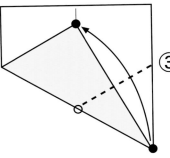

② Bring the lower left corner to the center line and fold. Make sure the fold goes through the lower right corner.

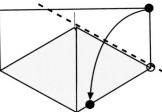

③ Bring the two points marked ● together and fold.

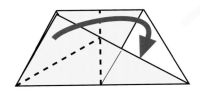

④ Fold along the edge.

⑥ Unfold back to a square.

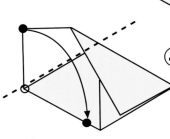

⑤ Fold along the edge.

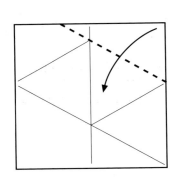

⑦ Fold along the existing crease line.

⑫ Fold in half and tuck the flap under the top layer.

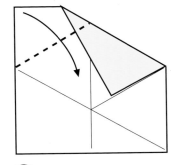

⑧ Fold along the existing crease line.

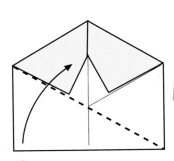

⑨ Fold along the existing crease line.

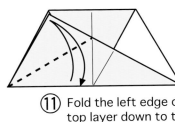

⑪ Fold the left edge of the top layer down to the bottom edge and unfold.

⑩ Fold in half and unfold.

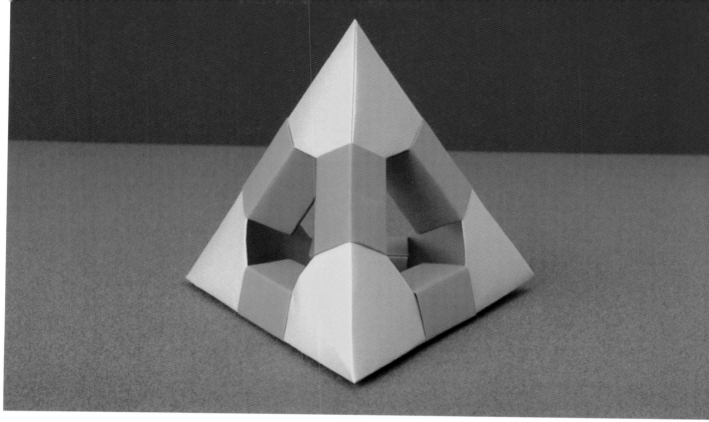

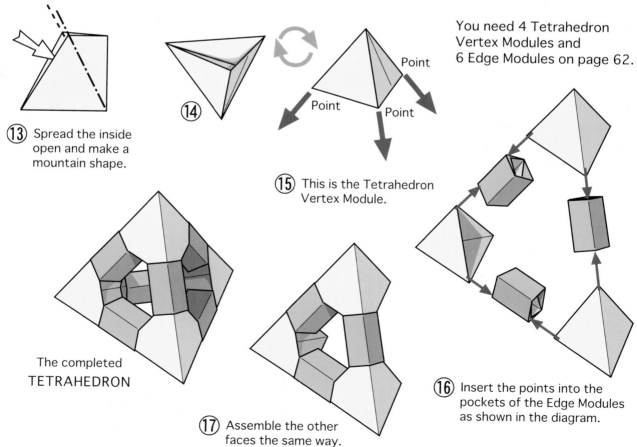

⑬ Spread the inside open and make a mountain shape.

⑭

⑮ This is the Tetrahedron Vertex Module.

Point
Point
Point

You need 4 Tetrahedron Vertex Modules and 6 Edge Modules on page 62.

⑯ Insert the points into the pockets of the Edge Modules as shown in the diagram.

The completed
**TETRAHEDRON**

⑰ Assemble the other faces the same way.

# POLYHEDRA KIT: OCTAHEDRON

You need 18 square pieces of paper, all the same size.

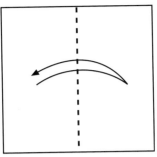

① Fold in half and unfold.

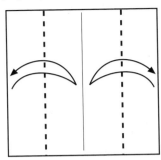

② Fold by bringing the right edge to the center line and unfold. Do the same on the left side.

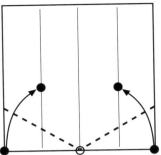

③ bring the lower left corner to the quarter line and fold as shown in the diagram. Do the same on the right corner.

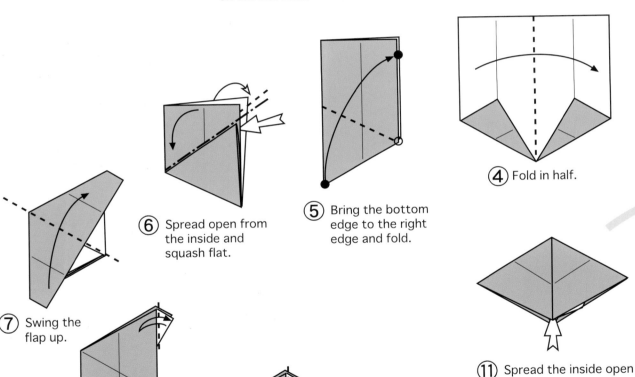

④ Fold in half.

⑥ Spread open from the inside and squash flat.

⑤ Bring the bottom edge to the right edge and fold.

⑦ Swing the flap up.

⑧ Fold the two flaps along the edge line and unfold.

⑨ Tuck the two flaps inside, under the top layer.

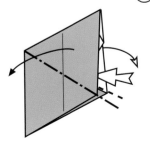

⑩ Spread open from the inside and squash flat.

⑪ Spread the inside open and make a mountain shape.

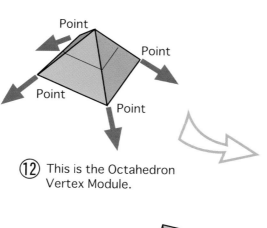

Point

Point

Point

Point

⑫ This is the Octahedron Vertex Module.

You need 6 Octahedron Vertex Modules and 12 Edge Modules on page 62.

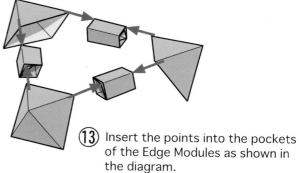

⑬ Insert the points into the pockets of the Edge Modules as shown in the diagram.

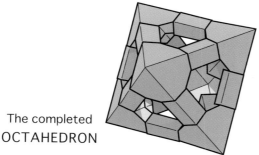

The completed
OCTAHEDRON

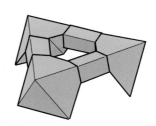

⑭ Assemble the other faces the same way.

# POLYHEDRA KIT : DODECAHEDRON

せい じゅうに めん たい

正 12 面体
*SEI - JUUNI - MEN - TAI*

You need 50 square pieces of paper, all the same size.

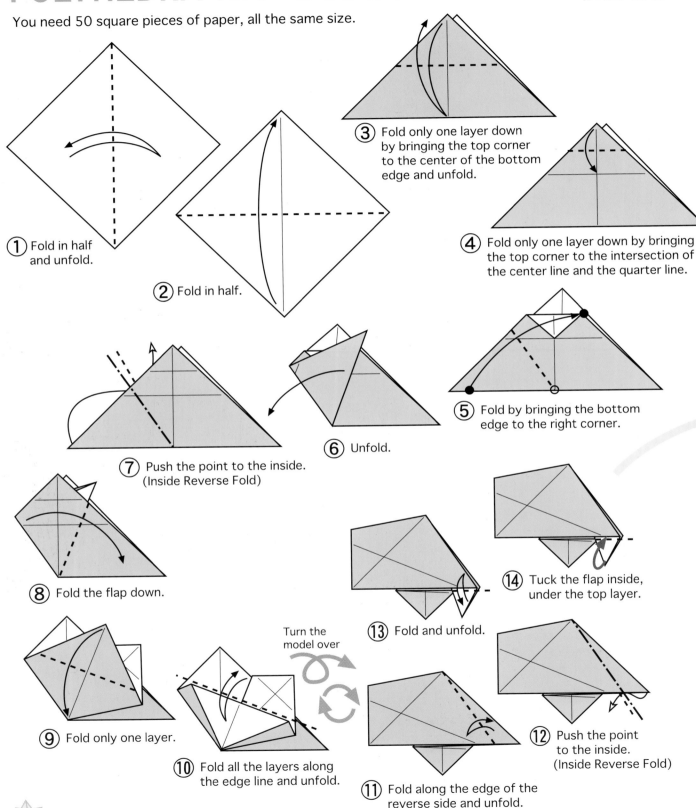

① Fold in half and unfold.

② Fold in half.

③ Fold only one layer down by bringing the top corner to the center of the bottom edge and unfold.

④ Fold only one layer down by bringing the top corner to the intersection of the center line and the quarter line.

⑤ Fold by bringing the bottom edge to the right corner.

⑥ Unfold.

⑦ Push the point to the inside. (Inside Reverse Fold)

⑧ Fold the flap down.

⑨ Fold only one layer.

⑩ Fold all the layers along the edge line and unfold.

Turn the model over

⑪ Fold along the edge of the reverse side and unfold.

⑫ Push the point to the inside. (Inside Reverse Fold)

⑬ Fold and unfold.

⑭ Tuck the flap inside, under the top layer.

⑮ Spread the inside open and make a mountain shape.

⑯ Fold along the three crease lines.

⑰ Fold a bit of the top corner down. Fold and unfold the tips of the side flaps so the flaps lie flush with the inside.

Turn the model over

⑱ This is the Dodecahedron Vertex Module.

Point

Point

Point

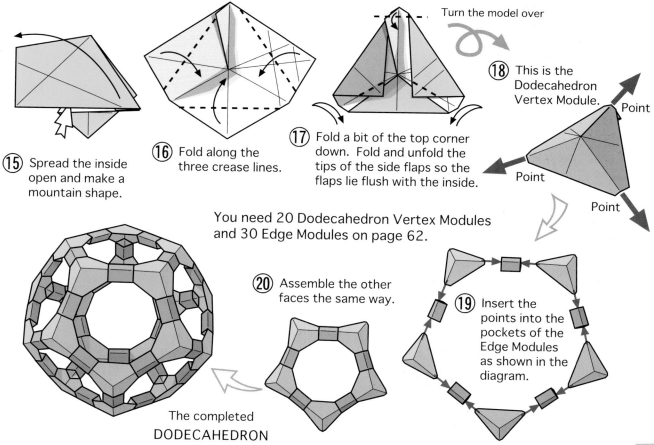

You need 20 Dodecahedron Vertex Modules and 30 Edge Modules on page 62.

⑳ Assemble the other faces the same way.

⑲ Insert the points into the pockets of the Edge Modules as shown in the diagram.

The completed
DODECAHEDRON

# POLYHEDRA KIT: ICOSAHEDRON

せい にじゅう めん たい
正 20 面 体
SEI - NIJUU - MEN - TAI

You need 42 square pieces of paper, all the same size.

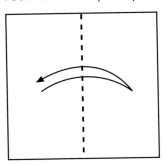

① Fold in half and unfold.

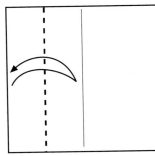

② Fold by bringing the left edge to the center line and unfold.

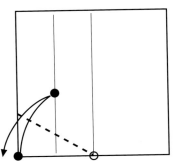

③ Fold by bringing the lower left corner to the quarter line and unfold as shown in the diagram.

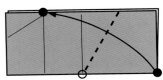

⑥ Bring the lower right corner to the top of the quarter line, marked ●, and fold.

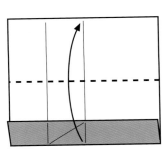

⑤ Fold the bottom edge up to the top.

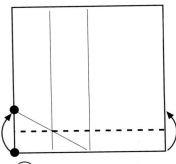

④ Bring the two points marked ● together and fold.

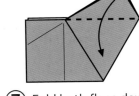

⑦ Fold both flaps down.

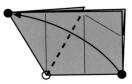

⑧ Bring the lower right corner to the left point and fold.

Turn the model over

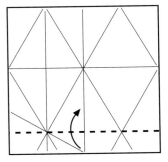

⑪ Fold along the crease line.

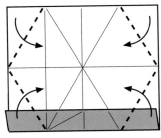

⑫ Fold along the four crease lines.

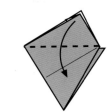

⑨ Fold both flaps down.

⑩ Unfold back to a square.

⑬ Make a dish shape by using the crease lines. The model becomes 3-D.

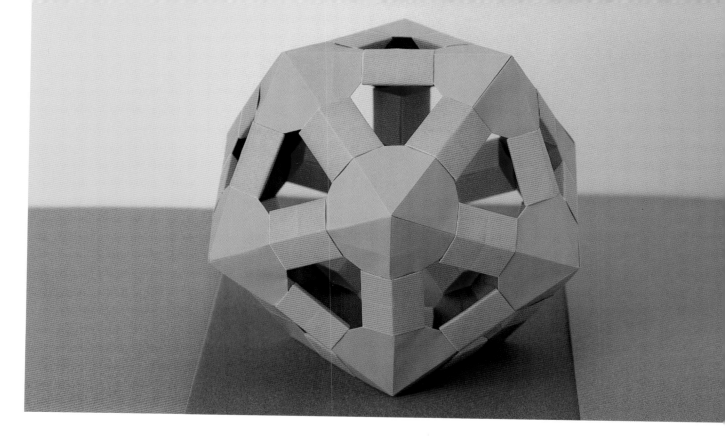

Turn the model over

Point

Point

Point

Point

Point

You need 12 Icosahedron Vertex Modules and 30 Edge Modules on page 62.

⑭ Tuck the flap under the layer.

⑮ This is the Icosahedron Vertex Module.

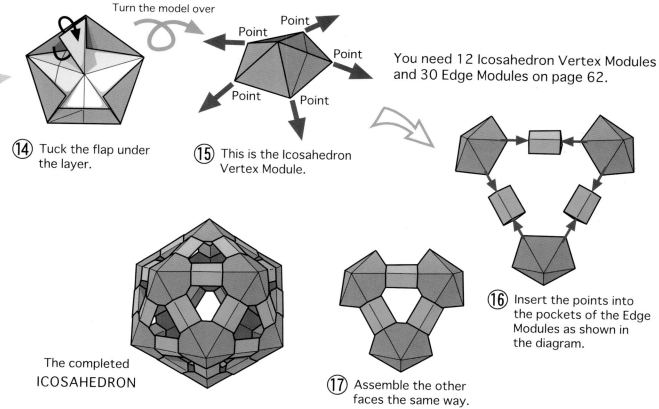

⑯ Insert the points into the pockets of the Edge Modules as shown in the diagram.

The completed
ICOSAHEDRON

⑰ Assemble the other faces the same way.

# STARS

## TRUNCATED ICOSAHEDRAL STAR
● Explanation: Page 87

## TRUNCATED OCTAHEDRAL STAR
Diagram: Page 85

## ICOSAHEDRAL STAR
● Diagram: Page 80

## TRUNCATED TETRAHEDRAL STAR
● Diagram: Page 83

## TETRAHEDRAL STAR
● Diagram: Page 76

## TRUNCATED CUBE STAR
● Diagram: Page 84

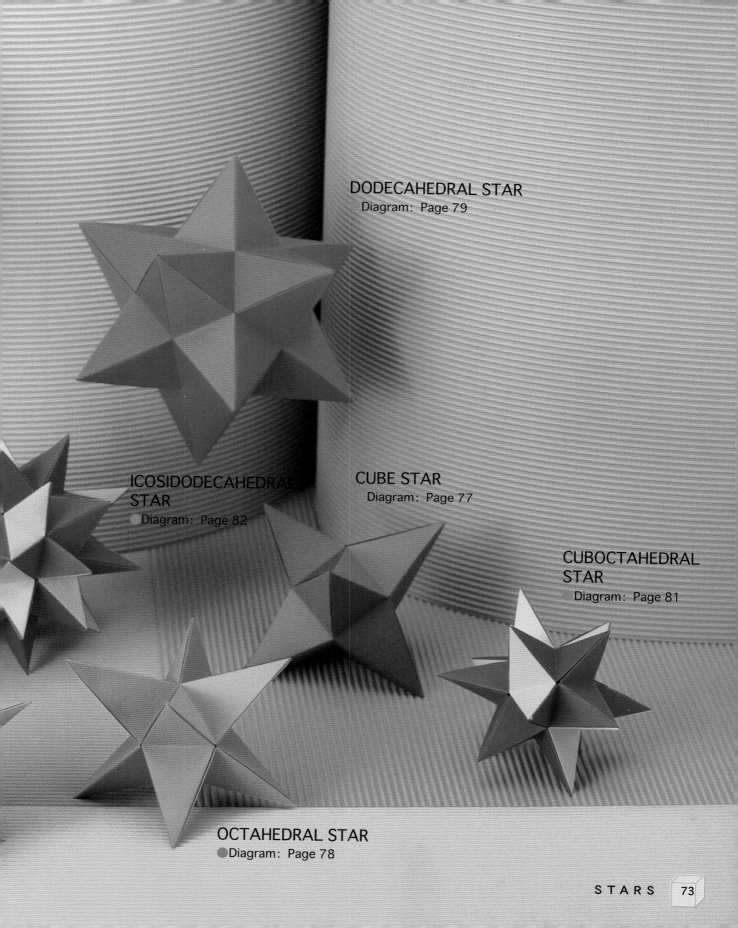

DODECAHEDRAL STAR
Diagram: Page 79

ICOSIDODECAHEDRAL
STAR
Diagram: Page 82

CUBE STAR
Diagram: Page 77

CUBOCTAHEDRAL
STAR
Diagram: Page 81

OCTAHEDRAL STAR
Diagram: Page 78

# STAR MODULE

星形のユニット
ほしがた の ゆにっと
HOSHI-GATA NO YU - NIT - TO

Start with a square piece pf paper.

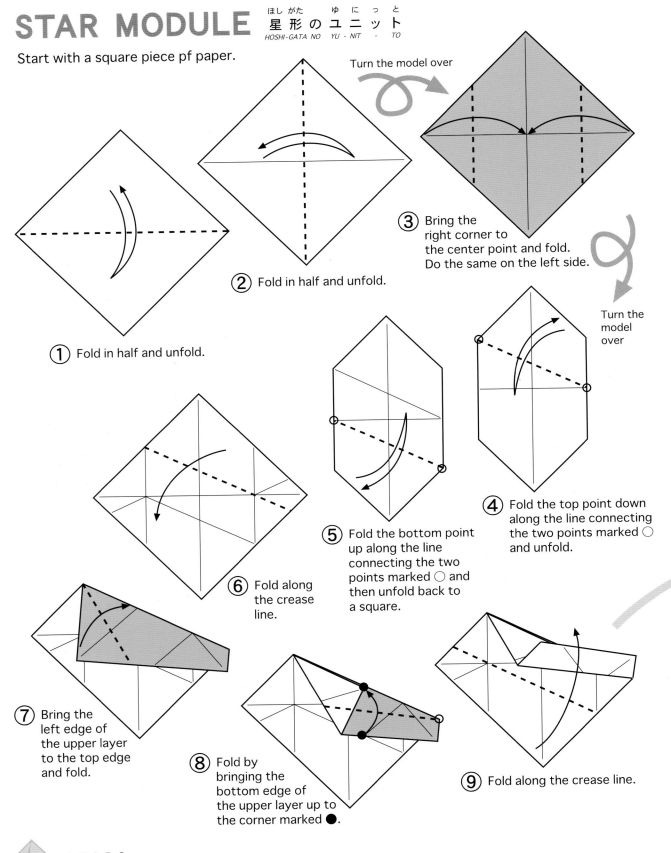

Turn the model over

③ Bring the
right corner to
the center point and fold.
Do the same on the left side.

Turn the
model
over

② Fold in half and unfold.

① Fold in half and unfold.

⑤ Fold the bottom point
up along the line
connecting the two
points marked ○ and
then unfold back to
a square.

④ Fold the top point down
along the line connecting
the two points marked ○
and unfold.

⑥ Fold along
the crease
line.

⑦ Bring the
left edge of
the upper layer
to the top edge
and fold.

⑧ Fold by
bringing the
bottom edge of
the upper layer up to
the corner marked ●.

⑨ Fold along the crease line.

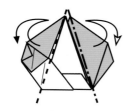

(16) Fold along the edges and unfold.

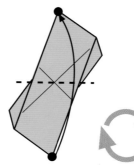

(15) Fold by bringing the two points together.

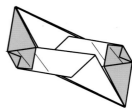

(14) Turn the model over.

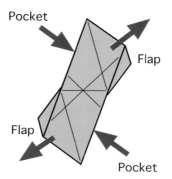

Pocket

Flap

Flap

Pocket

The completed
Star Module

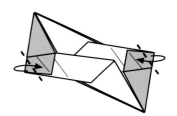

(13) Fold the two corners.

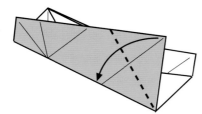

(10) Bring the right edge of the upper layer to the bottom edge and fold.

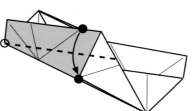

(11) Fold by bringing the top edge of the upper layer down to the corner marked ●.

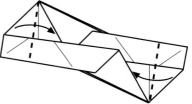

(12) Bring the right edge to the inside slanted edge and fold. Do the same on the left side.

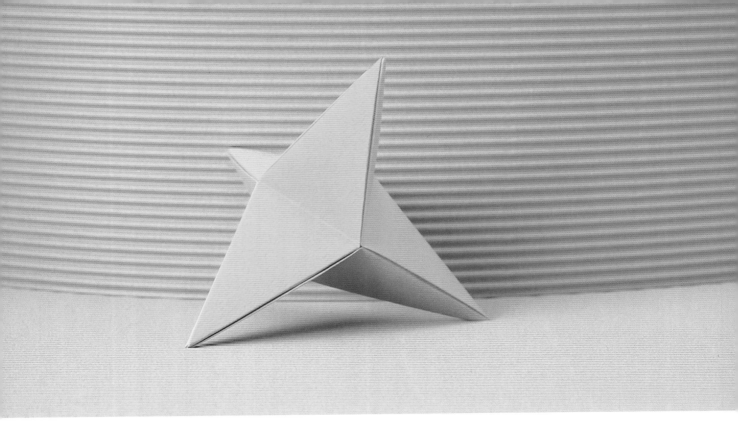

# TETRAHEDRAL STAR

You need 6 Star Modules on page 74.
(This model is unstable and will need some glue to hold together.)

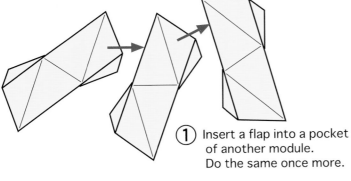

① Insert a flap into a pocket
   of another module.
   Do the same once more.

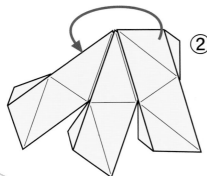

② Tuck the flap into the
   pocket and make a
   mountain shape.

③ Assemble the other
   three points as shown
   in the diagram.

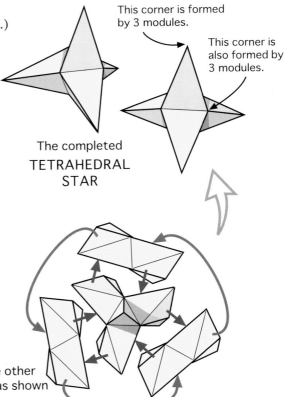

This corner is formed
by 3 modules.

This corner is
also formed by
3 modules.

The completed
TETRAHEDRAL
STAR

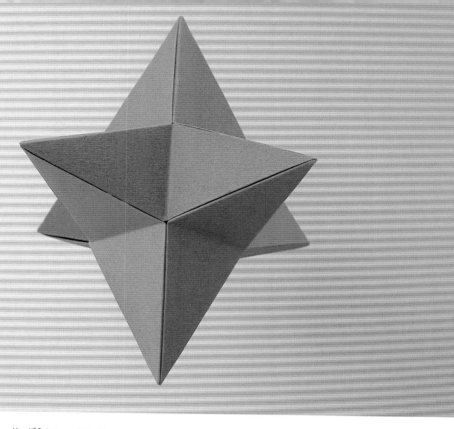

# CUBE STAR

りっぽうたい ほしがた
立 方 体 の 星 形
*RIP - POU - TAI NO HOSHI - GATA*

You need 12 Star Modules on page 74.
(This model is unstable and will need some glue to hold together.)

This corner is formed
by 4 modules.

This corner is formed
by 3 modules.

The completed
CUBE STAR

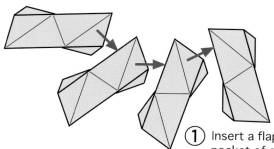

① Insert a flap into a
pocket of another
module. Do the same
two more times.

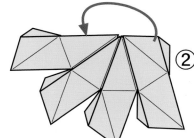

② Tuck the flap into the
pocket and make a
mountain shape.

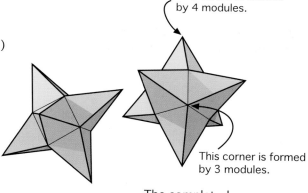

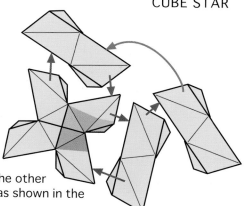

③ Assemble the other
five points as shown in the
diagram.

# OCTAHEDRAL STAR

せいはちめんたい　ほしがた
正 8 面体 の 星形
*SEI-HACHI-MEN-TAI NO HOSHI-GATA*

You need 12 Star Modules on page 74.
(This model is unstable and will need some glue to hold together.)

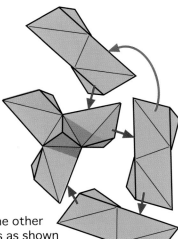

This corner is formed by 3 modules.

This corner is formed by 4 modules.

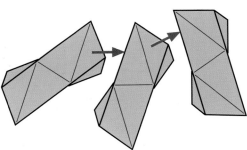

① Insert a flap into a pocket of another module. Do the same once more.

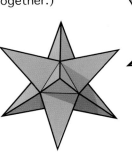

The completed
**OCTAHEDRAL STAR**

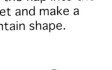

② Tuck the flap into the pocket and make a mountain shape.

③ Assemble the other seven points as shown in the diagram.

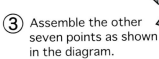

# DODECAHEDRAL STAR

正12面体の星形
SEI - JUUNI - MEN - TAI NO HOSHI-GATA

You need 30 Star Modules on page 74.
(This model is unstable and will need some glue to hold together.)

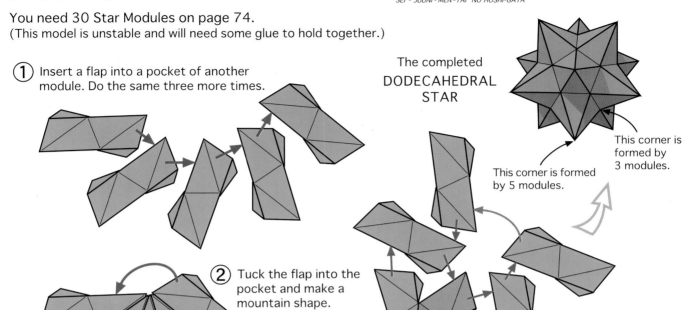

① Insert a flap into a pocket of another module. Do the same three more times.

② Tuck the flap into the pocket and make a mountain shape.

The completed DODECAHEDRAL STAR

This corner is formed by 5 modules.

This corner is formed by 3 modules.

③ Assemble the other 11 points as shown in the diagram.

# ICOSAHEDRAL STAR

せい にじゅうめんたい　　ほし がた
## 正 20 面体 の 星形
*SEI - NIJUU - MEN - TAI  NO  HOSHI-GATA*

You need 30 Star Modules on page 74.
(This model is unstable and will need some glue to hold together.)

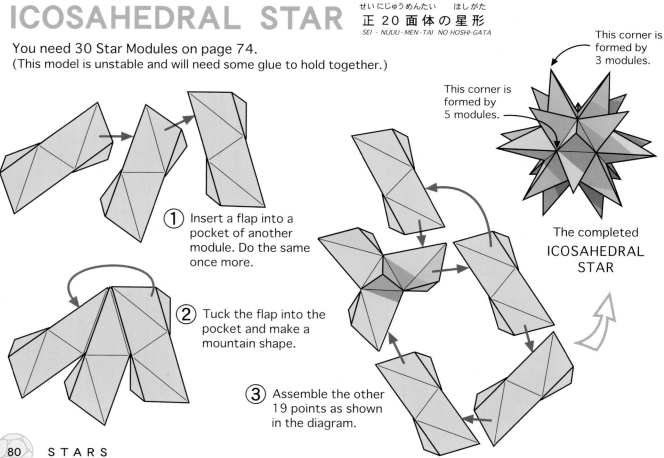

① Insert a flap into a pocket of another module. Do the same once more.

② Tuck the flap into the pocket and make a mountain shape.

③ Assemble the other 19 points as shown in the diagram.

This corner is formed by 3 modules.

This corner is formed by 5 modules.

The completed ICOSAHEDRAL STAR

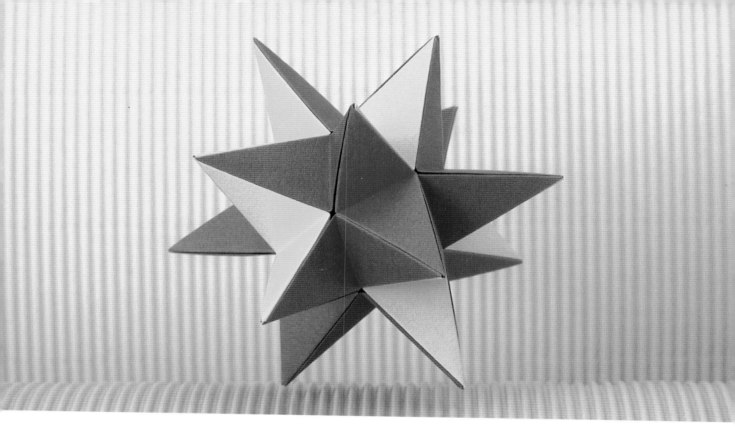

# CUBOCTAHEDRAL STAR

立方 8 面体 の 星形
りっぽうはちめんたい　ほしがた
*RIP-POU-HACHI-MEN-TAI  NO HOSHI-GATA*

You need 24 Star Modules on page 74.
(This model is unstable and will need some glue to hold together.)

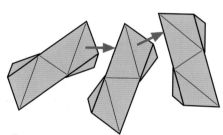

① Insert a flap into a pocket
of another module.
Do the same once more.

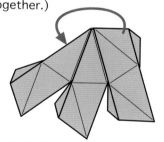

② Tuck the flap into the
pocket and make a
mountain shape.

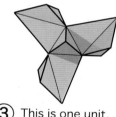

③ This is one unit.
You need 8 units.

Each new point is made
up of the flaps of 4 units.

④ Assemble the other
six points as shown
in the diagram.

The completed
CUBOCTAHEDRAL
STAR

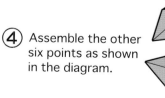

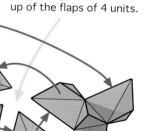

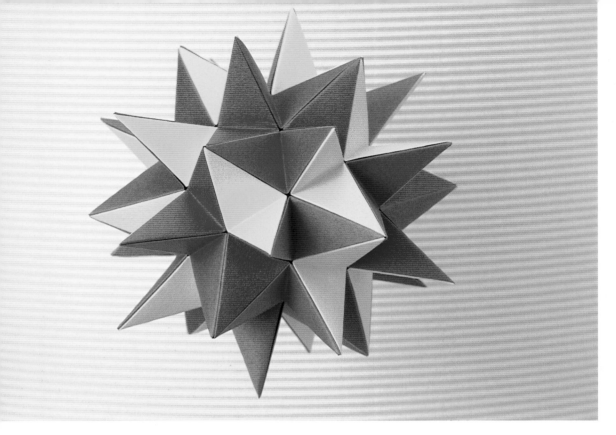

# ICOSIDODECAHEDRAL STAR

にじゅうじゅうにめんたい　ほし がた
## 20・12 面体の星形
*NIJUU - JUUNI - MEN - TAI  NO HOSHI-GATA*

You need 60 Star Modules on page 74.
(This model is unstable and will need some glue to hold together.)

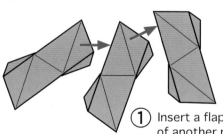

① Insert a flap into a pocket of another module. Do the same once more.

② Tuck the flap into the pocket and make a mountain shape.

③ This is one unit. You need 20 units.

Each new point is made up of the flaps of 5 units.

④ Assemble the other 12 points as shown in the diagram.

The completed
ICOSIDODECAHEDRAL
STAR

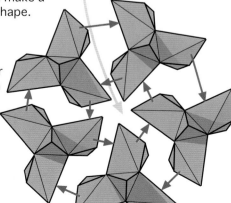

# TRUNCATED TETRAHEDRAL STAR

You need 18 Star Modules on page 74.
(This model is unstable and will need some glue to hold together.)

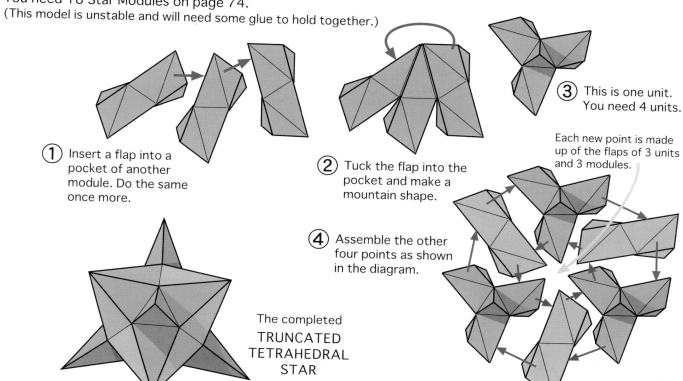

① Insert a flap into a pocket of another module. Do the same once more.

② Tuck the flap into the pocket and make a mountain shape.

③ This is one unit. You need 4 units.

Each new point is made up of the flaps of 3 units and 3 modules.

④ Assemble the other four points as shown in the diagram.

The completed
TRUNCATED
TETRAHEDRAL
STAR

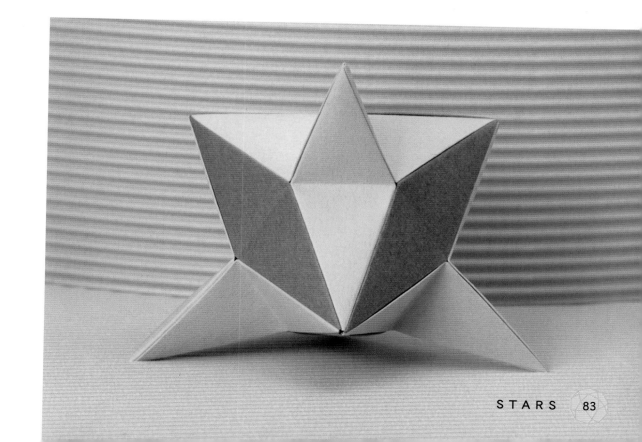

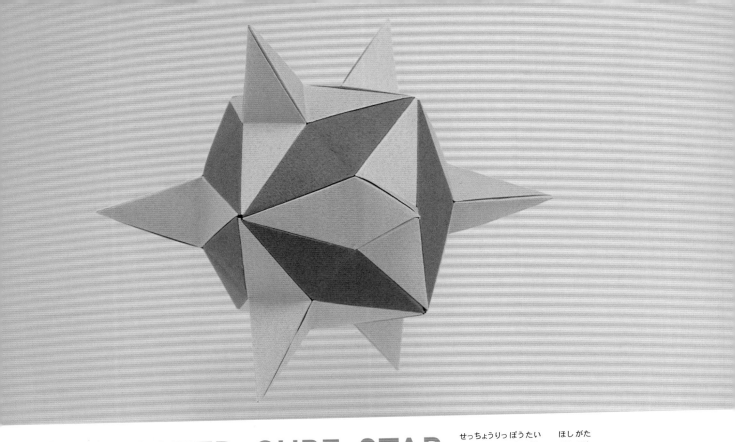

# TRUNCATED CUBE STAR

切頂立方体の星形
*SET-CHOU-RIP-POU-TAI NO HOSHI-GATA*

You need 36 Star Modules on page 74.
(This model is unstable and will need some glue to hold together.)

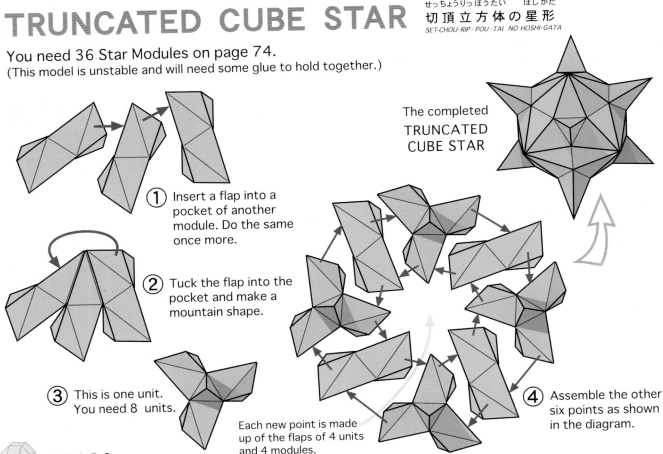

① Insert a flap into a pocket of another module. Do the same once more.

② Tuck the flap into the pocket and make a mountain shape.

③ This is one unit. You need 8 units.

Each new point is made up of the flaps of 4 units and 4 modules.

④ Assemble the other six points as shown in the diagram.

The completed
TRUNCATED
CUBE STAR

84 S T A R S

# TRUNCATED OCTAHEDRAL STAR

切頂8面体の星形
*SET-CHOU-HACHI-MEN-TAI  NO HOSHI-GATA*

You need 36 Star Modules on page 74.
(This model is unstable and will need some glue to hold together.)

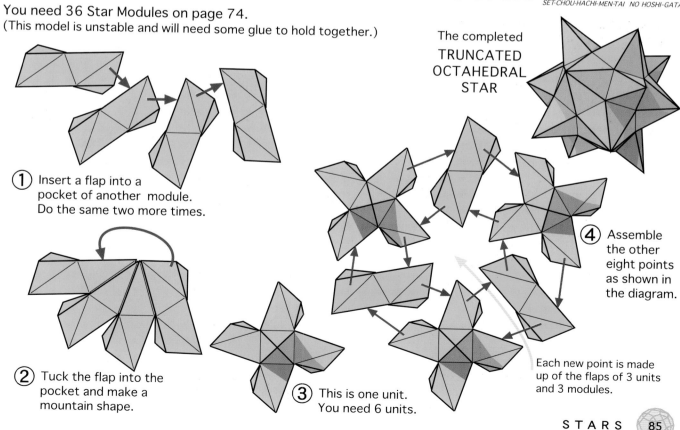

The completed
**TRUNCATED
OCTAHEDRAL
STAR**

① Insert a flap into a
pocket of another  module.
Do the same two more times.

② Tuck the flap into the
pocket and make a
mountain shape.

③ This is one unit.
You need 6 units.

④ Assemble
the other
eight points
as shown in
the diagram.

Each new point is made
up of the flaps of 3 units
and 3 modules.

# STAR POLYHEDRA

ほしがた た めんたい
## 星形多面体
*HOSHI-GATA-TA-MEN-TAI*

● We can imagine various star polyhedra based on the regular and semi-regular polyhedra. The method of making these star polyhedra is very similar to the method for making star polygons.

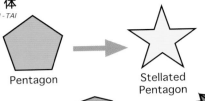

Pentagon → Stellated Pentagon

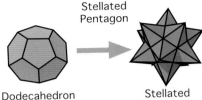

Dodecahedron → Stellated Dodecahedron

## Method 1:
By extending the edges or faces.
(This is called "Stellation")

● Polygon

① A polygon

② Extend an edge.

③ Do the same with the other edges.

A stellated polygon

● Polyhedron

① A polyhedron

② Extend a face.

③ Do the same with the other faces.

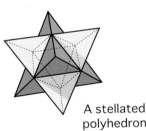

A stellated polyhedron

## Method 2:
By connecting the vertices or edges.

● Polygon

① A polygon

② Connect two vertices with a new line.

③ Do the same with the other vertices.

A star polygon

● Polyhedron

① A polyhedron

② Connect two edges with a new face.

③ Do the same with the other edges.

A star polyhedron

## Method 3:
By putting points on the edges or faces.

● Polygon

① A polygon

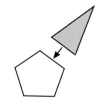

② Add a triangle shape to an edge.

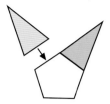

③ Do the same to the other edges.

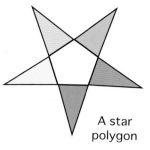

A star polygon

● Polyhedron

① A polyhedron

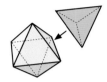

② Add a pyramid shape to a face.

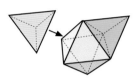

③ Do the same to the other faces.

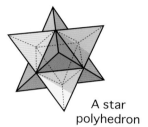

A star polyhedron

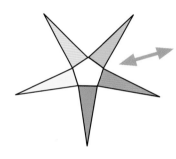

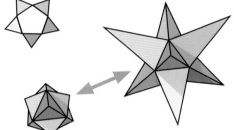

You can add a point of any size.

● There are many more kinds of stellated polyhedra. You can imagine and make various stars based on the tables on pages 28 and 29! For example, the star in the picture to the right was made with 90 Star Modules (see page 74) arranged as a truncated icosahedron.

## TRUNCATED ICOSAHEDRAL STAR

<ruby>切頂<rt>せっちょう</rt></ruby><ruby>20面体<rt>にじゅうめんたい</rt></ruby>の<ruby>星形<rt>ほしがた</rt></ruby>
*SET-CHOU-NIJUU-MEN-TAI NO HOSHI-GATA*

# FLUTTER WHEELS

FLUTTER WHEEL 1

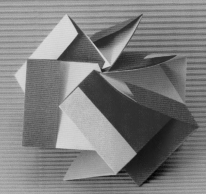

FLUTTER WHEEL 2

# FLUTTER WHEELS
すいしゃ
水 車
*SUI - SHA*

You need 6 square pieces of paper, all the same size for each type of model.

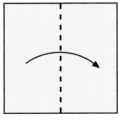

① Fold in half.

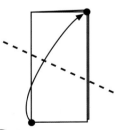

② Fold by bringing the two points together.

③ Unfold back to a square.

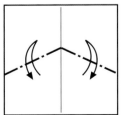

④ Mountain fold along the two crease lines and unfold.

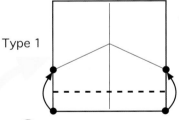

Type 1

⑤ Fold by bringing the two points marked ● together.

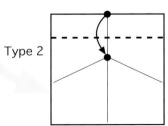

Type 2

⑤ Fold by bringing the two points marked ● together.

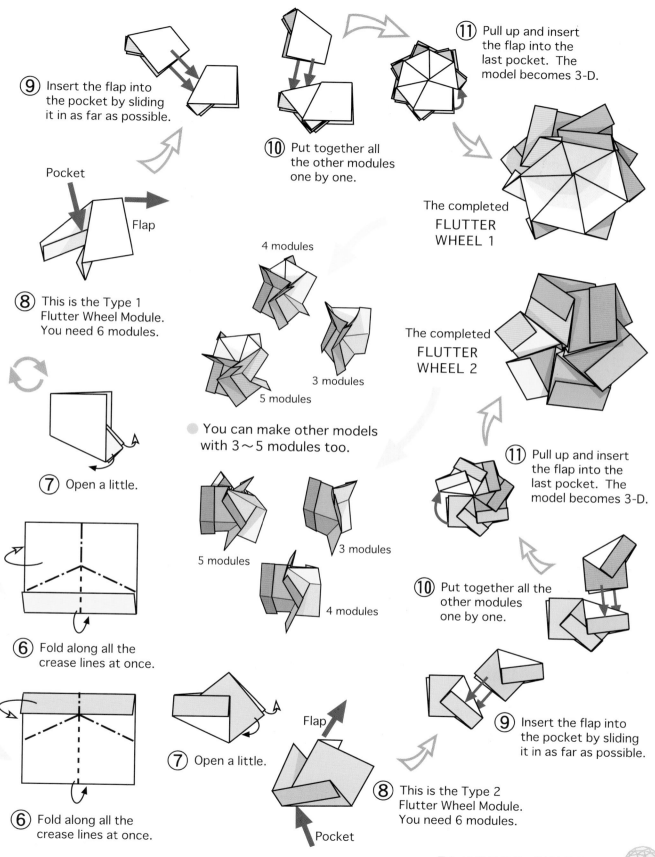

(9) Insert the flap into the pocket by sliding it in as far as possible.

Pocket

Flap

(8) This is the Type 1 Flutter Wheel Module. You need 6 modules.

(7) Open a little.

(6) Fold along all the crease lines at once.

(6) Fold along all the crease lines at once.

(7) Open a little.

Flap

Pocket

(8) This is the Type 2 Flutter Wheel Module. You need 6 modules.

(10) Put together all the other modules one by one.

(11) Pull up and insert the flap into the last pocket. The model becomes 3-D.

The completed FLUTTER WHEEL 1

4 modules

3 modules

5 modules

● You can make other models with 3〜5 modules too.

5 modules

3 modules

4 modules

The completed FLUTTER WHEEL 2

(11) Pull up and insert the flap into the last pocket. The model becomes 3-D.

(10) Put together all the other modules one by one.

(9) Insert the flap into the pocket by sliding it in as far as possible.

# Flutter Wheel Arrangements

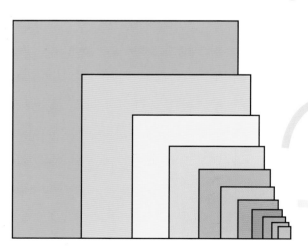

By gradually reducing the size of the Type1 or Type2 Flutter Wheel Modules (on page 88), you can create spiral shapes.

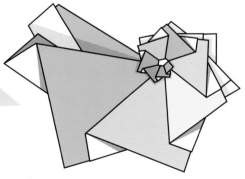

This spiral is made from Type 1 Flutter Wheel Modules.

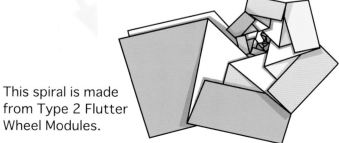

This spiral is made from Type 2 Flutter Wheel Modules.

# WINDMILL 風車
ふうしゃ
FUU-SHA

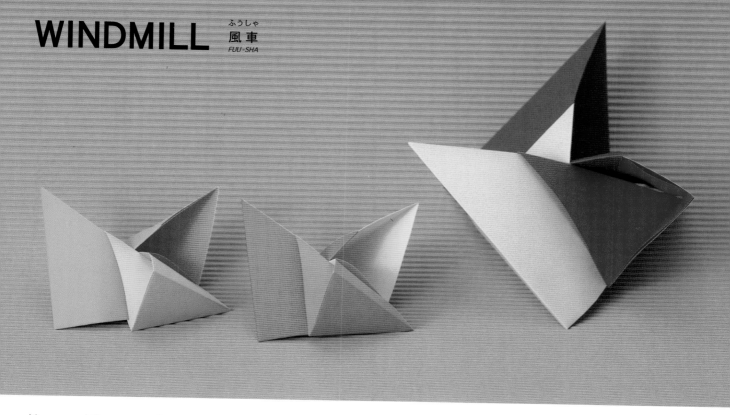

You need 3 square pieces of paper, all the same size.

① Fold in half.

② Fold in half and unfold.

③ Bring the right point to the top corner and fold.

④ This is the Windmill Module. You need 3 modules.

Pocket

Flap

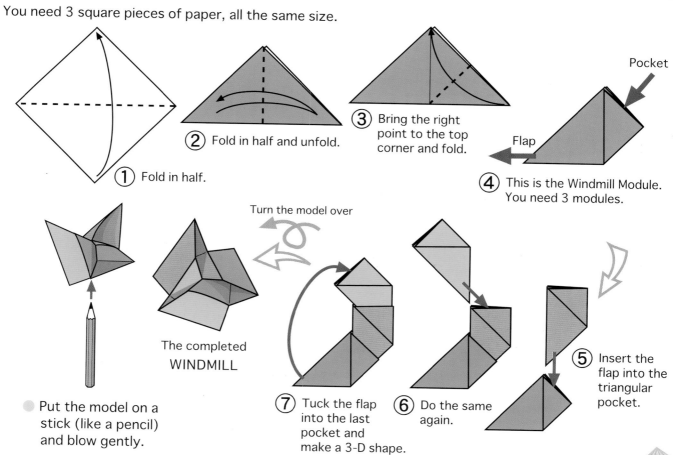

Put the model on a stick (like a pencil) and blow gently.

The completed WINDMILL

Turn the model over

⑦ Tuck the flap into the last pocket and make a 3-D shape.

⑥ Do the same again.

⑤ Insert the flap into the triangular pocket.

# SQUARE TILE 1　正方形のタイル 1
せいほうけい　たいるいち
SEI - HOU - KEI　NO　TA - I - RU ICHI

Start with a square piece pf paper.

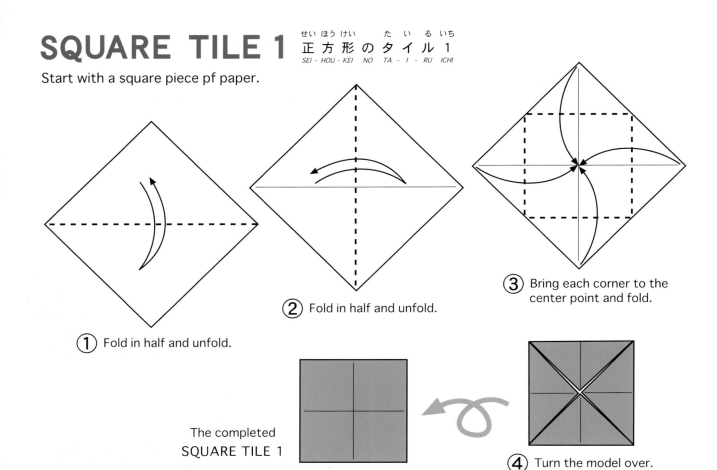

① Fold in half and unfold.

② Fold in half and unfold.

③ Bring each corner to the center point and fold.

④ Turn the model over.

The completed
SQUARE TILE 1

# RECTANGULAR TILE 1　長方形のタイル 1
ちょうほうけい　たいるいち
CHOU - HOU - KEI　NO　TA - I - RU ICHI

Start with a square piece pf paper.

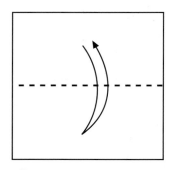

① Fold in half and unfold.

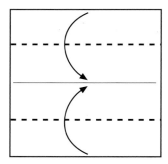

② Bring the bottom edge to the center line and fold. Do the same on the upper side.

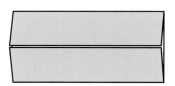

③ Turn the model over.

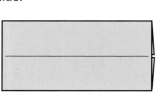

The completed
RECTANGULAR TILE 1

# RIGHT TRIANGULAR TILE

直角3角形のタイル
*CHOK-KAKU-SAN-KAK-KEI NO TA-I-RU*

Start with a square piece pf paper.

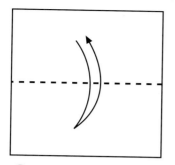 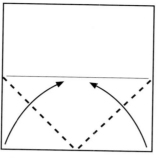 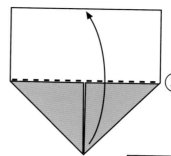

① Fold in half and unfold.

② Bring the lower right edge to the center line and fold. Do the same on the left side.

③ Fold the bottom corner up along the edge.

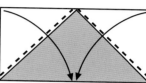

④ Fold the two corners down along the edges.

The completed
RIGHT
TRIANGULAR TILE

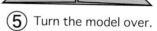

⑤ Turn the model over.

# ISOSCELES TRIANGULAR TILE

に　とうへんさんかっけい　　たいる
2等辺3角形のタイル
*NI-TOU-HEN-SAN-KAK-KEI NO TA-I-RU*

Start with a square piece pf paper.

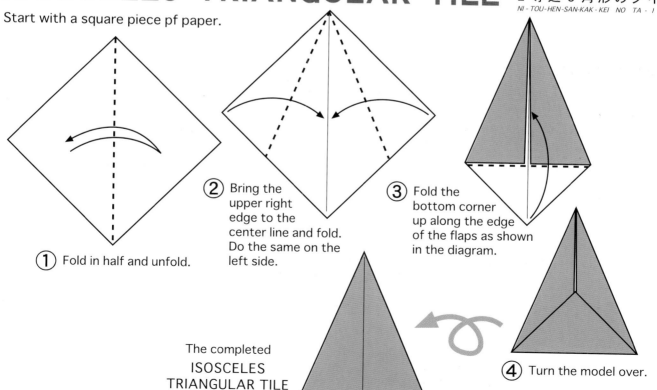

① Fold in half and unfold.

② Bring the upper right edge to the center line and fold. Do the same on the left side.

③ Fold the bottom corner up along the edge of the flaps as shown in the diagram.

④ Turn the model over.

The completed
ISOSCELES
TRIANGULAR TILE

TILES 93

# SQUARE TILE 2 正方形のタイル 2
せいほうけい たいるに
SEI - HOU - KEI  NO  TA - I - RU  NI

Start with a square piece pf paper.

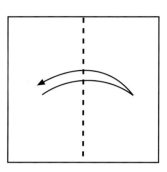

① Fold in half and unfold.

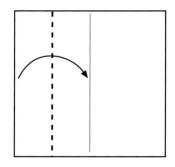

② Bring the left edge to the center line and fold.

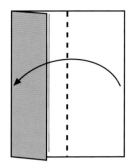

③ Bring the right edge to the left edge and fold.

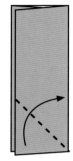

④ Bring the bottom edge of the top layer to the right edge and fold.

The completed SQUARE TILE 2

⑦ Tuck the flap into the pocket.

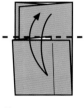

⑥ Fold along the edge and unfold.

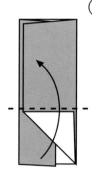

⑤ Fold along the edge.

# RECTANGULAR TILE 2 長方形のタイル 2
ちょうほうけい たいるに
CHOU - HOU - KEI  NO  TA - I - RU  NI

Start with a square piece pf paper.

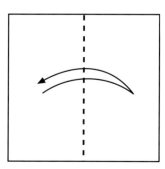

① Fold inhalf and unfold.

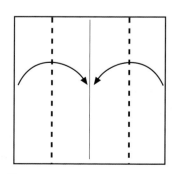

② Bring the left edge to the center line and fold. Do the same on the right side.

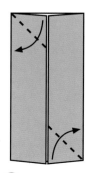

③ Fold only the upper layer.

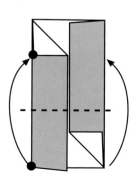

④ Bring the two points marked ● together and fold.

# REGULAR OCTAGONAL TILE

Start with a square piece pf paper.

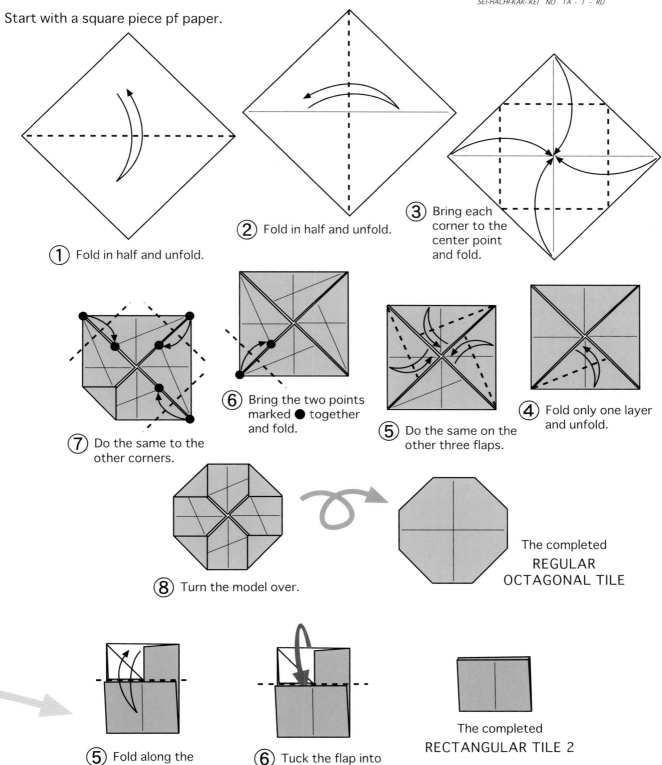

① Fold in half and unfold.

② Fold in half and unfold.

③ Bring each corner to the center point and fold.

④ Fold only one layer and unfold.

⑤ Do the same on the other three flaps.

⑥ Bring the two points marked ● together and fold.

⑦ Do the same to the other corners.

⑧ Turn the model over.

The completed
REGULAR
OCTAGONAL TILE

⑤ Fold along the edge and unfold.

⑥ Tuck the flap into the pocket.

The completed
RECTANGULAR TILE 2

# EQUILATERAL TRIANGULAR TILE

せいさんかっけい　　た　い　る
正3角形のタイル
SEI-SAN-KAK-KEI NO TA-I-RU

Start with a square piece pf paper.

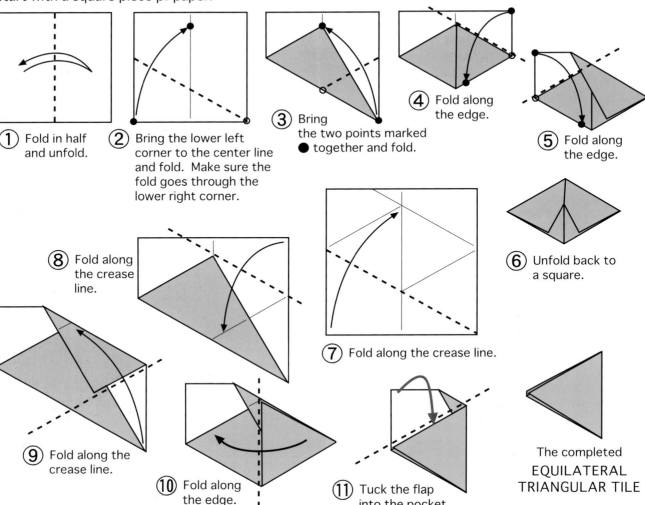

① Fold in half and unfold.

② Bring the lower left corner to the center line and fold. Make sure the fold goes through the lower right corner.

③ Bring the two points marked ● together and fold.

④ Fold along the edge.

⑤ Fold along the edge.

⑥ Unfold back to a square.

⑦ Fold along the crease line.

⑧ Fold along the crease line.

⑨ Fold along the crease line.

⑩ Fold along the edge.

⑪ Tuck the flap into the pocket.

The completed EQUILATERAL TRIANGULAR TILE

# RHOMBIC TILE

がた　　た　い　る
ひし形のタイル
HI-SHI-GATA NO TA-I-RU

You need a square piece pf paper. Start from step ⑦ in the above diagrams.

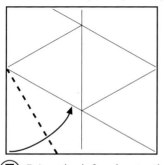

⑦ Bring the left edge to the crease line and fold.

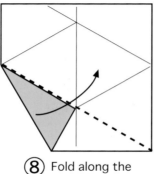

⑧ Fold along the crease line.

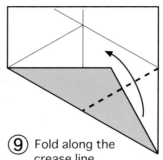

⑨ Fold along the crease line.

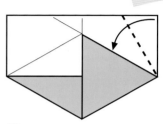

⑩ Bring the right edge to the upper edge of the top layer and fold.

# REGULAR HEXAGONAL TILE

せいろっかっけい　た　い　る
正6角形のタイル
SEI - ROK - KAK - KEI　NO　TA - I - RU

Start with a square piece pf paper.

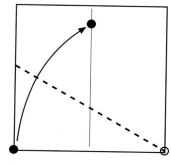

① Fold in half and unfold.

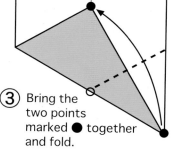

② Bring the lower left corner to the center line and fold. Make sure the fold goes throush the lower right corner.

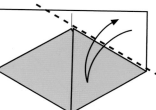

③ Bring the two points marked ● together and fold.

④ Fold along the edge and unfold.

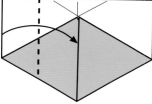

⑥ Bring the left edge to the center line and fold.

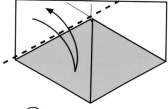

⑤ Fold along the edge and unfold.

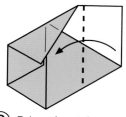

⑦ Fold along the crease line.

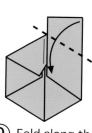

⑧ Bring the right edge to the center line and fold.

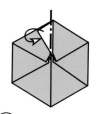

⑨ Fold along the crease line.

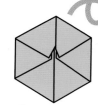

⑩ Tuck the flap under the layer.

⑪ Turn the model over.

The completed
REGULAR
HEXAGONAL TILE

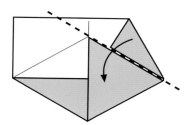

⑪ Fold along the crease line.

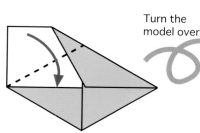

⑫ Fold along the crease line and tuck the flap under the layer.

Turn the model over

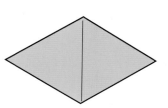

The completed
RHOMBIC TILE

TILES　97

# REGULAR PENTAGONAL TILE

正5角形のタイル
SEI - GO - KAK - KEI  NO  TA - I - RU

Start with a square piece pf paper.

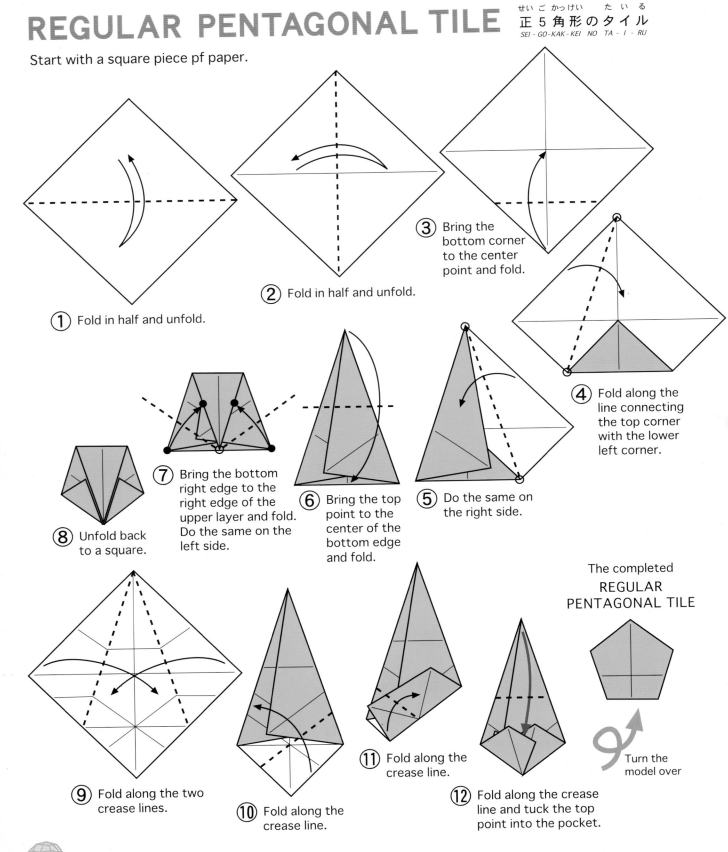

① Fold in half and unfold.

② Fold in half and unfold.

③ Bring the bottom corner to the center point and fold.

④ Fold along the line connecting the top corner with the lower left corner.

⑤ Do the same on the right side.

⑥ Bring the top point to the center of the bottom edge and fold.

⑦ Bring the bottom right edge to the right edge of the upper layer and fold. Do the same on the left side.

⑧ Unfold back to a square.

⑨ Fold along the two crease lines.

⑩ Fold along the crease line.

⑪ Fold along the crease line.

⑫ Fold along the crease line and tuck the top point into the pocket.

The completed REGULAR PENTAGONAL TILE

Turn the model over